*In the Beginning
There Were No Words*

The Universe of Babies

Caleb Gattegno

Educational Solutions Worldwide Inc.

First published in the United States of America in 1973. Reprinted in 2010.

Copyright © 1973-2010 Educational Solutions Worldwide Inc.
Author: Caleb Gattegno
All rights reserved
ISBN 978-0-87825-212-1

Educational Solutions Worldwide Inc.
2nd Floor 99 University Place, New York, N.Y. 10003-4555
www.EducationalSolutions.com

For all the children
who taught me so much
—and in particular
for Uma and Ashish
and their mother Shakti,
who made them blossom

Table of Contents

Preface 1

    Note to the Reader 3

Introduction: The Instruments for Study 5

1 Prenatal Preparation 15

2 Entering the World 31

3 Processing Energy 45

4 The Temporal Hierarchies 65

5 Talking 89

6 Speaking 105

7 Learning Other Things 141

8 The Love that Babies and Young Children Need 157

9 For the Education of the Very Young 173

Further Reading 187

Preface

Anyone who has gathered enough data about man's history will have noticed that that which is most fundamental, most primitive, is found last.

Men in the Western World after first finding themselves in the image of God and looking at life on Earth mostly as a way of attaining salvation in the next life, next collectively and individually moved to seeing themselves as nature's creatures, and after that as political and social creatures, until very recently they came to the realization that they are persons. Whatever one's place of birth, the creed of one's parents, the language one learns, the color of one's skin, the economic level of one's family and community, one asks today to be looked at as a person, complete at any age and in most circumstances.

Today, as persons, we reject the singling out of one feature or one item to define us, and we claim the right to be more ourselves as we change towards what our consciousness tells us we are, potentially.

Today we look at life, at the consumption of time by living, as a continuous process during which (to use the language that seems best to describe it) we objectify ourselves in our soma, where we manifest our perceptions and actions in accord with our (reachable) environment and in terms of our efforts to know our energy and its dynamics so as to get more from the mobilization of any amount of energy.

Today more and more of us see that man, the cosmic being who has reached the awareness of the singularity of himself as well as the uniqueness of each individual creature in the universe, is present from the start of each individual's being, in totality though not explicitly. The duality of being, potentially whole and objectively still in the making, results from our being in time, needing time to objectify, to change or transform what is possible into what actually is.

To be a person, to be (in the language of some) an individual, means that one makes oneself while living in time.

Man knows himself when he knows that what makes him one *also* makes the receptors of what his consciousness can reach in what he calls the inner and outer world. It is within the self that this distinction makes sense, but the unity between inner and outer is manifested every day to the point that it becomes very difficult to be articulate and clear concerning either a dual view of the world—the ego and the non-ego—or a monistic view which reduces everything to the set of inner impressions. We shall see examples of this difficulty in our discussion.

Preface

In this book what will be made articulate, and perhaps clear, is that by living our lives each of us constructs a manifested self and that full knowledge of ourselves, as the awareness of ourselves dwelling in time, is equivalent to giving the self the instruments for realizing its potential.

What has all this to do with the life of babies, the subject of this book?

Each of us as a baby has contributed mightily to all his subsequent manifestations. To know ourselves as babies opens for us—all mankind—a wide door towards a much brighter future. What babies are in fact, needs to be known as truth; but the owning of that truth transforms our lives as do love, illumination, good luck or deep sorrow.

The transformation is at the level of awareness, and when this new awareness permeates all our functionings we find ourselves different from what we were, perhaps incomparably more powerful.

Note to the Reader

Some people who read the manuscript of this book have told me that they find the first chapter the most difficult to grasp. I was reluctant to move it from its logical position at the beginning of the study but I advise readers that they may find it does not give up its secrets easily and they may therefore prefer to begin their study with other parts of the book returning to the first chapter when they are more familiar with the instruments I use in every chapter.

The last two chapters of this book concern the assistance adults can give in the education of young children and therefore will sound more like recommendations than statements of fact.

Caleb Gattegno
New York City
April 1972

Introduction:
The Instruments for Study

When I was born, like everybody else I must have looked as if I only knew a few things—sleeping, eating, crying and evacuating.

This is what outsiders could say and probably did say of me because appearances dictated these conclusions.

But little did my parents know that I was working hard to learn to do all those new things I had never done before.

Parents indeed do not know what they themselves as children did with their time, nor what their children are doing with their time. Parents are too busy doing that which needs doing for themselves and their charges, including the newly born child, to watch what the reality behind the appearances is and to understand the use of time by babies.

In this book we shall ask ourselves some hard questions and if we can answer them in an acceptable manner, we shall perhaps know something about our own remotest past, which continues to be the present for those who need still to be engaged in each of the vital activities demanded of young babies for their survival.

The first thing for the reader to understand is that there are questions that are never asked before a certain moment, when someone becomes sensitive to an aspect of reality. Thus, all men on Earth up to a certain time were unaware that their planet was "round," or that air had weight, or that the moon always showed us the same side because its rotation around its axis takes as long as its revolution around the Earth, or that electricity could be produced, etc.—until someone ascertained that each of these things was so. But once they were ascertained, the truth belonged to all and could be reached by anyone willing to pay the price for knowing the procedures required to establish these truths.

Although no one can remember his birth, his early childhood, his embryonic life, it is possible to arrive at definite knowledge in these fields. Until now, such certainty has been reached by developing some "objective" approach borrowed from the exact sciences and biology.

In this book we shall add to these methods some others which are suggested by the problems we shall study. Their value for the reader will perhaps be found in that they manage to open up a vast number of fields for exploration and also give us some guidance in the field of education and the human sciences.

The questions we shall ask to help us in our task are:

- *when did we start doing this or that?*
- *could we know how to do this without having to spend some time learning it?*
- *how could such learning take place? Does it need some functionings before it starts? If so, which ones and what are they in detail? When were they acquired?*
- *are there any activities that need only oneself? (If there are, we shall know that to understand them the intervention of the concept of environment will not be needed.)*
- *are there any activities that, while needing only oneself, do not need to be completed at birth or do not need to be transmitted by "heredity"? (If there are, we shall have distinguished them from those that seem to require genes and chromosomes to account for them.)*
- *are there any activities present both in utero and ex utero and that therefore serve to link the individual's life that is visible to observers to the portion that is normally hidden? (This question may make us more perceptive of the significance of prenatal life for each of us.)*
- *are there any instruments that enable us to understand the demands of life at all stages, opening up the details of all such stages in a manner needed for that understanding? (If such*

> *instruments exist, they are in competition with those that are already exclusively used in some fields, and in those fields we can test by contrast the usefulness of the one against the other.)*
>
> - *if there are such "vertical" instruments, which unify life at its different moments, are there other instruments that cover for each of us a "horizontal" layer of manifestations? (If they exist, they must be compatible with those that have to be integrated in one's life. Both kinds of instruments are necessary if we would explain the tremendous actual variety of human experience.)*

Because we want to understand babies, who have neither been studied seriously enough nor known intimately enough, we must demand of ourselves a discipline that is new.

It is so easy to use "blanket explanations" in order *not* to understand, that this is what most people do on many occasions. For example, we use the word "naturally" in certain of our answers to cover up the fact that we have not seriously asked a particular question (such as, say, "Why growth?"); or the word "imitation" without knowing whether imitation is at all possible.

The discipline consists in stopping for a moment and examining whether we are really in contact with the challenge.

Here is an exercise to indicate in precise terms what we mean. Many people say "Children learn to speak by imitation" and are convinced it is true. If they really want to know whether it is true, they should ask themselves, for example, what they mean by imitation. Do they mean that a baby *sees* what a speaker does with his throat or tongue and then reproduces these actions? Or do they mean that if this use of oneself were known to a child it would be easy for him to do what others do, although in fact he only *hears* people in the environment speaking and what the child must do is not hear but speak?

Neither alternative is imitation as it is generally understood by those who use the word, yet such people do not criticize the content of their mind when they give their opinion on this matter.

No one can learn to speak by imitation simply because we hear with our ears and speak with our vocal system. The one system is submitted to the given impacts from the environment and the other is a totally voluntary system. In addition, we each speak with our own voice while hearing the voices of others, so how can there have been imitation?

We shall hence have two jobs: (1) demand of readers that they stop repeating what circulate as accepted explanations but do not ensure understanding, and (2) develop some correct means for understanding.

Only thus have we any chance of granting ourselves the knowledge of what we actually did (or do) with ourselves as babies (or at any time) in order to know something or to own a skill that stays with us all through life.

Perhaps a powerful beginning can be made if we realize here and now that wherever we go we carry ourselves and that what we move about is "contained in a *bag*", of which our skin is a token.

This bag separates the space within from the space without (even if one day we find that it also links these two). In our bag we have what we made *in utero*, since we were born with our bag and with a content in it. But we also carry much that we cannot at once see as matter, although it is movable from place to place—our memories, our moods, our skills, our imagery, our vocabularies and grammars, our loves, our projects.

This concept of the bag is an important instrument of our investigation, and it must be used in order to become useful. Readers who want to uncover its value could start by seeing whether this awareness supplements or contradicts others held by them.

All the items studied by anatomists, physiologists, neurologists, embryologists, etc., are in our bag. Hence, if we want to remain true to reality, we are bound to respect whatever truth these observers have found. But, supplementing the results of their investigations, we must also place in our bag our perceptions, our habits, our thoughts, for they too can be transported like our bones, muscles, and organs, wherever we go. Our religious views, our tastes are in our bag as are our sentiments, feelings, resolutions, etc. Our fears and our darings, our enhanced sensitivities and our blunted ones, our panoramic views of history, mythology, some sciences and languages, are also there.

Besides cataloguing and classifying the enormous number of items we find in our bag, we can find, if we examine them, that they are united, linked, related selectively, and this in turn puts in our bag the individuality, the integrity, the uniqueness of each of us, the sum of what we have done with ourselves and what we could do.

If the bag defines the individuality, what goes on inside it defines all sorts of inner lives. The various ways our bag relates to that which is not it and that which is in it, will define its life in the world.

Because we can find that soon after conception there is a membrane enclosing the developing embryo, we can see our manifested items displaying arrangements in space, connections and transformations in time, chemical and physical organizations, and we could be satisfied with a description of all this. Most books on the shelves in specialist libraries prove this point.

But there is more inside our bag. There is a nervous system, a brain, and a spine made of cells, called neurons, and all the nerve endings everywhere on the inner side of the bag. There are sense organs linked with the central nervous systems (the hemisphere and the cerebellum) and ductless glands linked to the lower and middle brain. Now, during the *in utero* development, while the specialized tissues are being made (and which end up being available to oneself, as can be proved by the voluntary character of the muscle tone and the capacity of an individual to scratch or not to scratch, even when a message along the nerve reveals an itch), during this time we have to assume that there is a way of knowing what goes on in the development and construction of the somatic self. The alternative position is to trust in continuous miracles. So a description of arrangements, connections, and so forth, is not enough.

In this book, one of the tools for understanding ourselves as babies is to recognize the existence of a continuing property of the self, one which is known by all at different stages in life—*self-awareness*. If I can know at this moment what I want to write down but do not know in the same way how I hold and guide the instrument for writing, there was still a time when I had to conquer the skill of writing and be totally absorbed in it to achieve its mastery. Both activities are the result of self-awareness. In a similar way, my not knowing *now* what I did to reach such a thorough knowledge of my skin that it now permits me to coordinate the acts needed to chase or crush an insect creating a sensation on my neck or back—which set of actions I channel to my brain through my sensory nerves—will not preclude that I did work consciously to become aware of how to interpret messages before entering into an action. The development of the somatic self—that is, *in utero*—is accompanied by a process of awareness.

However reluctant readers may be to adopt the assumption that somatic consciousness has been as vivid and as well known to the self as social or intellectual consciousness is today, I suggest that they entertain it for a while in order to find out what help it provides in understanding babies, or for that matter any age and any condition.

One feature of this new instrument of research that puts the self of each of us in the most intimate contact with the forms usually studied from outside, and places consciousness in an active and searching state in contact with all it does, is that it makes it possible to use one and the same language at the somatic, mental, and spiritual levels.

It also makes it possible not to patronize people or distort activities that the investigator does not or cannot identify with. For as soon as we accept that consciousness is at work from the start, we know (1) that we are concerned with a person, and (2) that if we think of each of us as an organism moved only by laws of nature, we do not see all. We make room for the singularities of every individual. We introduce a powerful rectifier of over-simplistic generalizations and make room for a retraction of any statement, each of which was provisional in any case. *Relativity*—required by the mere existence of viewpoints associated with systems in motion with respect to which there are observers—and *evolution* which merely expresses that time affects everything although in definite ways—are to be blended with consciousness to give us the capacity to embrace the unique, changing reality of each-of-us-in-the-world.

With these powerful instruments we shall glean important crops and justify *a posteriori* the method of approach to babies offered in this book.

Of the many challenges faced by students of babies we shall select those that seem today the most critical to educators and to parents, in so far as they want to educate themselves so as to educate respectively their charges and their children.

Educators in this context are those who elect to work with others so that they will be able to meet the future as routinely as they meet the present—where the latter is synonymous with living life consciously and is routine only through the continual learning that takes place.

We shall conceive of each person as a learning system that does not need to be motivated externally in order to acknowledge perceptions and become engaged in actions. The system contains its own dynamic. It is also a learning system that is changed by the learning already achieved and that therefore has the capacity to encounter new perceptions and become involved in new actions, which in turn affect and change the system.

One of the jobs of education is to hook itself up with all these different learning systems and provide each person with what is compatible with the spontaneous involvements of his individual self, while at the same time producing an expansion of the consciousness of that self so that it can live more abundantly. Until recently this job was performed by chance and intuition. We think it can become deliberate and sustained because we are now able to know much better what the task entails and how to carry it out.

1 Prenatal Preparation

It takes only a few days or weeks for parents to know whether a fertilized ovule is growing into a future baby. And the knowledge comes from the changes in the mother's condition which signal that the environment in which the baby will grow is adapting to its needs.

Embryologists have studied a number of aspects of this growth, and any biology book will re-state how the egg, made of the fusion of an ovule with a spermatozoid, starts and pursues a dual process of subdivision and growth that leads to the specialized tissues and then to the organs.

Molecular biologists have asked deeper questions and have wanted to understand how each moment of growth can be described in chemical terms, that can then be ascertained by chemical tests. Since the content of cells is complex and since the chemistry of the simplest living organism far exceeds the processes that the most sophisticated chemical factory is engaged in, there is need for a very sharp intelligence to grasp the phenomenon of growth at this level. But since an amoeba or a bacterium manufactures its chemicals in apparently identical ways from one individual to the next, the explanatory schemas offered by scientists are confused. On the one hand scientists acknowledge that each individual organism must make itself from material that is less complex than itself and obtainable from the environment, and on the other, that the complex process of synthesis must be given in advance, in the individual as it were, so as to produce an individual or a particular species. The various blue-prints are said to be passed on from generation to generation as inscriptions on the hereditary stuff called DNA and on the items called genes that affect each particular state.

For our purpose here it is perhaps permissible to break down a schema that uses a language only specialists understand. From the environment, i.e. from his mother, the unborn baby of any species receives the ingredients that the blood of his mother brings to him. This blood, however much it is affected by the reaction of the mother's organism to the semi-foreign body hooked onto the wall of her uterus, is the same as that which she uses in her own cells. Her cells are already completed and are serviced in certain ways by the content of the blood. But the embryo's cells have to be constructed, and the complex substances of the cells must be synthesized by the embryo itself out of the existing substances that form its present somatic stage and those that are in the mother's blood. What if this blood is deficient in some substance? The embryo must either produce it or take the consequence of its absence by not being able to do some jobs that other specimens do normally. Similarly, if the mother's blood carries some chemicals not needed for the pursuit of the embryo's development, the embryo must either filter them out and protect itself from them or suffer the consequences of having to integrate unnecessary elements.

It is clear that the relationship between a mother and her embryo is not a simple one, or a perfectly predictable one, or one that does not offer the possibility of leading to unique individuals. In fact *no two living organisms can be identical* though they can be identified for some purposes.

In the case of human beings, whose diets may differ considerably more than those of other living creatures, the mere dependence of the embryo on the content of the mother's blood introduces a variable that may radically change one offspring from the next. If the synthesis of chemicals that form the contents of the cells in the various tissues is simultaneously conditioned by the raw material available and by the possibility of hosting some chemical reactions but not others, we can in fact see each individual as working at the formation of his own chemical self, and we will not talk as if all the processes were governed by "natural laws."

People who speak of "the embryo" are appealing to a metaphysical entity: "The embryo develops as instructed by a ready-made program conditioned by the DNA of the first cell." This seems a legitimate statement for anyone describing only the appearances.

Every embryo is indeed endowed with a program that continues a species. But every embryo must also synthesize itself out of material which it does not control and which may be deficient or redundant in the chemicals required. Though it is possible to offer a description of embryonic development that uses the plausible language of blueprints of reactions and chemicals (as is done almost universally), it is also possible to develop an alternative language to describe the embryo's work at the prenatal level that will reveal the compatibility of this work with the self-determination of the individual at later stages.

The dual movement of cell growth and then subdivision, followed by growth, followed by subdivision, and so on, until tissues are formed; then another dual movement out of which the organs (or functional tissues) are constituted; and then another which develops specific functionings—this dual movement of elaboration and utilization we shall find all through life, in the acquisition of skills in particular.

If in later life I find I have criteria that tell me to continue the elaboration rather than the utilization of part of myself (and the functionings that belong to that part), I can also see that the jobs to be done in utero obey the same requirements. However little was given to me in the egg, it nonetheless was sufficient to make me capable of using it to give myself a form that remains with me as an intrinsic part of myself—as indeed with any skill developed during this period. (We separate ourselves from our forms and functionings only when they appear to us inadequate for some jobs, to all of which we are linked through consciousness.)

The fact that consciousness is present in cells and tissues is forced upon us when, for example, we alone are presumed to be

1 Prenatal Preparation

able to locate a dysfunction for a physician. He can then hook on to what we tell him the intellectual schemas that express what he knows from the outside.

From outside, each of us *has* "a body;" from inside we *are* what we have called "a soma". The difference is simply that *our* consciousnesses are at work in our somas, whereas our bodies are objects to be considered like all other objects. In the medical schools of the West, much of what future doctors study is learned in morgues where consciousness is no longer present, or in operating theaters where it is prevented from manifesting itself. The assumption of consciousness is not made, though the truth is that no learning, and so no growth, can take place without it.

Rather than retell the history of the soma as the description of somatic growth, let us trace the working of consciousness on the stuff that will supply it with a working form. This is the meaning of a stretch of life spent *in utero* as a preparation of the self for the *ex utero* future.

Before moving into this let us note two points:

1. A still-born baby has had a life, which means a consciousness, even if his social and other lives did not manifest themselves. The stretch of time taken for the transformation of his energy into a somatic structure is the expression of both that life and the consciousness. The expectation of further time for *that* life comes from other people, people who

swerve from meeting what they do not understand and take refuge in beliefs.

2 The appearance of a baby "monster" or a "handicapped" baby can lead to family tragedy or untold moral pain over years only through the interference of legitimate, though unwarranted, expectations from adults. If all babies have to make themselves out of the program contained in DNA and the stuff provided by the mother, they prove that they can use their time *in utero* to perform the very complex task of producing their soma. It is with this form and its functionings that, like all of us, they have to live their life, not the life of someone able to give himself a different soma.

From outside we all look as if we were enclosed in our bags and that we manifest ourselves in what is perceived as its content. When some people found muscles and bones in each bag, they provided a model of man that could move around. As other people found lungs and a heart, the model became more complex, and respiration and circulation were added to it, with their respective functions of oxygenation of the blood and combustion of food stuffs in the cells (to produce the energy to maintain the body's temperature and to cope with locomotion). The digestive tract, as the supplier of broken-down chemicals for both storage and the elimination of waste was added. Others discovered the nervous system and its refined sensitivities. Others found hormones and the functions of glands, and other vitamins and enzymes as the catalysts of the many chemical reactions performed continuously by all organisms. Still others found that the psyche acts on the functions and organs to transform them, and so the psyche was added to the arsenal of instruments for understanding man.

1 Prenatal Preparation

The movement of these "uncoverings" was clearly away from immediate appearances towards less and less obvious elements—which were nonetheless always there in the examined somas (examined either as bodies or somas)—thereby complicating indefinitely the model of ourselves we had to carry with us if we wanted to understand ourselves.

Clearly we do not acquire enzymes or hormones as we grow older or only after a certain stage of development. Not only are they there from the start, but much of what molecular biologists added to our knowledge of man (and animals) is the outcome of the recognition that the subtle activities of enzymes are indispensable to the production in the embryo of the various proteins that will specialize the cells into tissues and organs. Some scientists have tended to locate in the egg all the potential for growth that other scientists have shifted to the brain. But since the egg precedes the constitution of the tissues which will become the brain, the material that is in the egg conditions the sort of brain and the kind of functionings that are possible.

How does one explain why one thing and not another happens in the embryo?

As an organism developing, there are functions not asked of me (such as speaking a language) and others that I cannot postpone (such as structuring my organs). Hence I shall not give any time to what is irrelevant and give all my attention to the task on hand—in the sense that we give it to study, in the sense that I give it to the task of writing this, closing myself to all distractions by putting my consciousness in a pinpointed way within the synthesis of years of somatic awareness so as to hold the pen and force it to design these and no other words, a polarization of energy towards writing and no other non-automatic work. Consciousness is energy.

All my attention, at the level of the embryo, means that there is an alternation of intense conscious elaboration followed by a consolidation of the result, using as little consciousness as is required in order to survey it and to signal any dysfunction to the much larger portion of consciousness that has been freed from the task of elaboration. This is followed by a shift towards the elaborated form that is now available for new tasks, which in turn gather all one's attention to do that which is required to produce the next "automatism," a structure that maintains itself with an absolute minimum of consciousness, thereby in its turn freeing the self for more complex tasks using what is available, and so on.

Man begins with one single cell, like amoebae or bacteria, because life can take that form, as proved by these organisms. As a single cell it is not a man, but since the single cell has the capabilities (not yet fully understood in the case of multicellular organisms) that permit it to use time to gather chemicals to maintain life, the living egg begins a human life at the somatic level and transforms itself so that in every one of us the functions of the egg are still alive, as are all their transformations.

The enormous jobs—of making proteins by combining the amino acids brought by the flow of mother's blood with both the enzymes already in the egg and those in the blood, of alternating the fine controls that produce a stoppage of growth at precise moments and then the start of subdivision followed by new growth, of letting some chemicals take over that control—all this is the conscious life of the embryo. No part of the soma is formed without the active presence of consciousness manifesting itself at every moment as an extremely sensitive chemist, extremely knowledgeable about what is required and how to achieve it with the supply of chemicals from the mines of the mother's blood and the egg. (Recycling, a notion of much popular concern today, is one of the embryo's techniques since the same enzyme can serve to produce any amount of the same protein, although each enzyme can produce only one particular kind of protein.)

One key aspect of this model is that consciousness as energy finds that it can produce extremely effective dynamic structures by delegating to supervisory systems the maintenance of these structures, thus using very little of itself, enabling it to be present in each segment of the soma without having to immobilize itself. Automatisms (objectified energy) are the answer to demands for efficiency. Through a feedback device they maintain the automatic sections within the reach of consciousness and its immediate intervention.

Our soma is a "responsible" display of the functioning of our consciousness as manifested in the organization of residual energy into a closely-knit network which controls the reception of chemicals, their distribution, their storage, their recycling, their repair and their elimination. All these controls are made from scratch with raw materials that have to be processed by "knowing" delegates of consciousness, which remain to monitor once the task is deemed correctly completed.

The role of the parents in the original endowment of the living egg out of living gametes does not preclude an egg from transforming that endowment beyond recognition.

The role of the environment is relative or supreme according to the ability of the embryo's self to cope either totally or not at all with the supply of material taken to it by the mother's blood.

Though mainly engaged in producing its soma *in utero*, there are very many additional jobs for the self in that stretch of time. Indeed, that a fetus can be born prematurely and survive without an umbilical cord tells us that for many weeks it must have been doing something with itself other than just building its body in its mother's womb.

What each of us did in the two phases of making all the specialized tissues, and of making these belong to the self for the particular functions they perform best, provides each baby at birth with a stupendous arsenal of somatic functionings.

We shall see in the next chapters how consciousness takes advantage of both the existence of such sophisticated organizations and of their functions in a manner not unrelated to what has been happening *in utero*, but we shall return here to the acquaintance each of us has with the soma in the making.

As soon as the energy of the self has been objectified in tissues and some additional energy committed to them to energize them and link them to the self, the tissues become the keyboards on which the self plays its variations. These variations are *compatible* with the objectified energy because they are variations on that energy.

In the case of muscles, the self needs only to remain consciously in contact with the muscle tone—which is semi-free energy in the sense that it can be added to or subtracted from, but remains in contact only with the muscles. After the stage of objectifying the muscles, consciousness is only required to be present in the form of muscle tone, which is immediately accessible to the will. As some muscles—the so-called involuntary muscles—are involved in functions which need adjustment less often, observation of the muscle tone in these cases is delegated to special organs that look after them most of the time for most of our lives. Some of us pay the price of reaching the muscle tone of these muscles by disciplining ourselves inwardly and thus prove that "involuntary" muscles, no less than voluntary ones, are integrated in the self that made both.

Our brain and our nervous system have been objectified at a certain stage in the mobilization of energy for the production of the soma. Like all other parts of the bag they are objectified energy and their various components, produced in time, satisfy various requirements of consciousness capable of knowing itself as soma.

The fact that the lower and middle brain are more concerned with functions involving the mobilization of large amounts of energy than the upper brain, and put this energy into the control of some organs and some functionings, while exemplifying again the process of consciousness delegating power to some of its feedback systems, also shows that consciousness has managed to construct an adequately complex system to maintain contact with all its objectified elements.

The brain is man's instrument for keeping him informed all the time of all the vicissitudes of the objectified elements. It is consciousness objectified to free the self by taking over the tools of all the functionings that form part of the objectified self.

Our brain does very many things (but not all—it does not make itself). It is so intimately linked with the objectification of the soma that, *in utero*, whenever a tissue is given a structure and a function, it notes them and keeps in contact with them—as both energy objectified and also energy vitalizing them. Organs are being watched in every cell in every one of their functionings.

And most of this work is the work done by the baby before birth. And because we do not see it done we assume that it is either not taking place or is done by a transcendental power called "necessity," or "heredity," or even "God."

Since the embryo has worked mainly at the objectification of organs and at checking that the flow of energy into them is adequate to tell him that their functionings are compatible with the universe of the womb, we can understand that every not-yet-born baby has a full life *in utero* even if he becomes deaf or blind or handicapped after birth. That child *in utero* is a "normal" unborn baby, having performed his "normal" duties—the duties, in particular, of knowing the extent to which he can affect his muscle tone, or can perceive an impact on the organs and localize it, or can work on nerve endings to command a selected movement, or can perform the changes that do not need outside stimuli (such as contracting the tongue, displacing the uvula, or epiglottis, opening or closing the larynx, eyelids, lips, rectal sphincter) and be sure that each element does what his will commands.

An unborn baby of any species has not only performed many activities that require learning but has managed to show that he knows how correct learning can be carried out in a number of fields. He has for so long and so effectively been in contact with different molecules, synthesizing them using the proper catalysts, that he is endowed at birth with knowledge of himself as a molecular cosmic being. Some very young children refuse some foods, using their opposition to the pressure from their environment in a way similar to the way they used to filter unwanted materials present in their mother's womb, or similar to their elimination of unwanted chemicals through urination and defecation. To assume molecular awareness in all living beings, man included, is to continue a function that was necessarily undertaken by the embryo and the fetus. Man is a molecular being and is therefore submitted to all physical phenomena which, by definition, involve molecules.

What we have learned at the embryonic stage goes much further than having equipped ourselves to be sensitive to the realm of molecules entering into chemical reactions. We are sensitive to variations in field energy since fields exist in the universe of matter. All those fields present within the bag must have been known by our awareness as it was polarized by receiving the actual changes taking place. If electrons are free to move in the bag, in its space, or in the organized channels (nerves, veins. . .), or in the organs, the electromagnetic fields generated by these electronic displacements must be perceptible to the self—as would be any impact upon their normal manifestation by a disturbance that can reach the inside of the bag.

Because consciousness before birth is obviously nonverbal, it is manifested by what consciousness can do at the level of involvement it is at. Just as we saw that it can realize what is required at the molecular level and effect it, we must accept that the newborn baby is aware of the electromagnetic inner reality and can cope with it in those forms it has experienced. Among these are the electricity in the muscles and in the brain. But there are others, such as exposure to X-rays from outside sources or other radiations, perhaps still unknown to scientists, that may be beyond its power to deal with and may lead to disturbances that affect the self before birth in unforeseen ways.

If mothers after their own birth develop an electromagnetic shield to protect the inside of their bag from the outer electromagnetic disturbances that take place in the surrounding universe, it may be unnecessary for the embryo to do likewise. As part of the inside of the mother's bag it may be *ipso facto* protected. But it is also possible that the bag of the fetus needs protection from electro-magnetic changes inside the mother's womb.

Another non-verbal awareness permitted to each not-yet-born-baby is the formation of the so-called *body-image*. Under this name, for a long time, has been understood the image each of us has of every part of his soma, the intimate knowledge of his limbs, say, which remains in the mind even after an amputation.

During the period of life *in utero* the nerve endings that map the bag onto the mind have been made so that they inform the self of any and every alteration that takes place on its surface (as say, later, the skin informs the self of a pin-prick). This inner knowledge of the bag is so primitive that no one needs to become aware of it as such, but can become conscious of it later in life in a number of circumstances, thus making the body-image an instrument of self-knowledge in the world.

In this regard, to show that one can know one's body-image without recognizing it, we shall cite two observations very often made. One concerns the spontaneous drawings of young children which display features of themselves, though they are not aware of it. (Many artists continue this kind of drawing particularly when drawing or painting by imagination.) The other concerns the large number of married couples who look alike even before meeting each other and living together: people seem to be led in their taste by their body-image.

Again, it is probable that able surgeons' competence in performing some operations is not only based on study and practice but also on this inner knowledge of the contents of the bag. Agreement between their study of the anatomy of the body and their knowledge of their own body-image, non-verbal as such knowledge is, must facilitate their intimate knowledge of anatomy and physiology.

To sum up this chapter we can say that the instruments mentioned in the introduction for the investigation of this field have been used and have allowed us to see that the preparation for life in the womb consists of the recognition, never to be achieved again, that we are molecules, cells, tissues, organs, chemical and physical entities shot through with (non-verbal) awarenesses that permit the integration of what is to come with what is.

Because awareness of variations of energy is accessible, our self becomes sensitive to what can be dynamically stabilized and thus keeps a check on functionings. Dysfunctions call for the intervention of consciousness—and the knowledgeable self that has learned what its soma is all about knows what to do to put things back into balance.

To know that one has to act on muscle tone and not the muscles is part of what we bring into the world outside the womb; to know that there is an entry into the depth of one's soma is another; to know that some functions of the brain are delegations from the self to subtle cybernetic systems energized by the self for the control and maintenance of its structures is still another; to know that one is more than one's soma, is another.

2 Entering the World

Even though the space of the womb is part of the universe we shall call the complement of that space the world. Until birth no one knows who the baby is, not even the mother who dearly loved him while helping him to make himself.

So when the baby is born we have a very different set of questions to work on. Because observations are now easier, many facts can be picked up which will help us to understand what babies do with themselves in the first few weeks of life.

It is of this stage in life that the popular saying about babies is apparently true: that babies sleep most of the day, that they cry when they wake up, that they eat and evacuate and do not seem to have any other concern. That this appearance is fallacious will follow from the study in this chapter.

Indeed, since the environment has changed radically at birth, the newly born baby now has a number of new functions thrust upon him. He must take air through his lungs and oxidize his blood himself. Because his food was formerly processed by his mother and sent to his system through the umbilical cord, now that this is cut he must take in his own food through his mouth and process it to the levels his functioning organs are used to. So he must learn all that the digestive tract will do from now on, which his mother unconsciously had done for him until now.

In the womb he was held by a cushion of liquid and now he lies on the kind of bed his culture supplies for babies: soft or hard, certainly harder than the womb.

He will be covered and dressed according to the requirements adults impose, and he has to learn to adjust to these demands.

He did not have to inhale until now, and now his nose may have to cope with particles that affect his skin and produce new behaviors (responses to the environment) that have to be known before they can become adequate.

The unsophisticated belief that all this is acquired by instinct is certainly out of place in understanding the newly born baby.

If we know that the vigilant self of the baby, which has done so much prenatal work, is still vigilant and ready to use what it is and what it has to adjust to the challenges encountered, there will be no need for a miraculous entity like instinct to be called in to understand what babies do with themselves after birth.

There being no need for the embryo to process pressures from the outside while in the womb, its sense organs have been made but have not been activated. In the womb, sensory nerves are made of bunched-up fibers that can transmit only an overall impact to the centers. For a time after birth, consciousness is still, so to say, refused to these nerves. However, all others are active—in particular those that command the peristaltic movements of the digestive tract whenever the ingested food touches it.

The lips must learn to hold on to the nipple. Then the muscles of the mouth must pump liquid with the lips, and while the liquid is in the mouth, the tongue must hold it so that the epiglottis closes the opening of the trachea (with the vocal cords) and the uvula closes the passage to the nose. Then the tongue must bend to deliver the liquid to the esophagus. All these new demands must be learned quickly and well, for the burning of reserves will create an imbalance requiring replenishment.

Mother's milk is mainly water to begin with, and so the rest of the digestive tract will not have much to do at this time. After a few meals the baby masters sucking, swallowing and the coordination of the demands of breathing and swallowing.

Because pumping is voluntary and since the self can interpret both the impacts on the various parts of the mouth and the functioning of these parts, an alert consciousness handles the matter on the whole without hitches and gives the impression of an innate predetermined and inherited behavior. But even this impression does not quite stand, for we shall soon find the limits of this attack on the new demands from life.

Of course breathing must be mastered at once, and its automatic functioning is established in the first few moments of life in the world. In the womb, the three thoracic muscular systems used for breathing were made ready to function as voluntary muscles. In the world, they are helped by the influx of the first gulp—made possible by the pressure of the surrounding air and the vacuity of the lungs. Soon after this first gulp the return of the muscles to their previous state pushes some of the content of the lungs out, but a small amount of carbon dioxide in the air activates the nerve that controls the tension of the diaphragm, creating a pull on the pressurized air that is in the atmosphere. And the cycle begins again. From then on, as the expulsion of carbon dioxide brought by the blood to the lungs brings a sufficient amount of carbon dioxide to keep things going, the breathing becomes rhythmic and seems unrelated to the voluntarity of the three muscular systems, which nonetheless remains.

At the prenatal stage the heart pumped the mother's blood into the arteries to irrigate all the tissues, including the lungs. But it did not have to receive oxidized blood as it is doing now. Thus, the new functions of the lungs are, first, this oxidization, which requires that air be pumped-in in sufficient quantity to change the hemoglobin into oxyhemoglobin, and second, the expulsion of the carbon dioxide produced by the combustion in the cells occurring in the previous phase. Because the lungs were not functioning in the womb, all the oxidization had been done by the mother, together with the elimination of the waste via the incoming and outgoing flow of blood.

The heart itself goes on as before, but the blood that returns from the lungs and, as before, is sent into the tissues, is oxidized in the lungs, making breathing a new vital function.

Consciousness is required to learn to avoid taking air into the digestive tube when swallowing one's food. For months the newly born baby struggles with learning this task. Adults may still have a problem with it, and some cultures allow belching as an acceptable way of restoring the separation of eating from breathing.

As the days go by and the food becomes more consistent, the different phases of digestion need to be practiced.

Saliva is produced in the mouth in quantities not yet under control. In the stomach the gastric juices are mixed with the salivated food and the reflexes are triggered by the presence of matter in the cavity and its contact with the glands in the walls. Prepared but not yet functioning, the various parts of the digestive tube begin to learn to respond to the varying composition of the mother's milk that partially replaced the substances drawn from the mother's blood. Some of the reserves in the liver, the spleen, and the marrow are called in while the digestive functions are made to work properly.

The waste from the cells, instead of being directed to the umbilical cord, must now go to the bladder and the large intestine, and there too, there are new functions to learn.

Since there is normally no continuous evacuation, we must conclude that a certain degree of habituation to the accumulation of waste takes place quite early. The sphincters are voluntary muscles and they are closed and opened at will. In the beginning of life in the world it is entirely an inner decision of the baby that keeps them closed or open. Later this decision will be coordinated with other considerations and lead to the abandoning of diapers.

The baby who takes in what his mother gives him from her breasts or from bottles has no control any more on what he filters or accepts. He learns to throw up, he develops diarrhea or constipation to cope with the unknown chemical composition of his food when it does not agree with him. He may refuse to eat when his sensors recognize some chemicals that are not acceptable to his state. Even the care of "nature" that is at work in the metabolism of the mother cannot altogether ensure that the milk offered the baby will not trigger rejection by him in one form or the other.

Thus, there is plenty to learn during the first few weeks, and during that time the baby is intensely engaged in new vital jobs that have just come his way.

Crying is a form of activity used by all babies as soon as they are born. It comes about because of what is available to them from their previous stage. It is not aimed at the environment, though the people in it consider it a call for help. But the baby is not aware of the existence of this help. Crying comes to him as a form compatible with his state and only later will it be used as a tool to relate to the people around in the way they expect.

Many mothers have been at a loss to understand why their baby cries so much. Some babies do not indulge in crying. Some even do not cry at all for a long time, and parents may consider them to be subnormal. The vast majority of babies do cry. Some cry for a certain duration at the same hour every day for some months for no reason understandable to anyone.

There are various cries which have different significances for the crier and the people around. Let us first look at crying as originating in the baby and afterwards link it with the other forms originating in the environment.

When air passes through the larynx, the voluntary vocal cords can control its emergence from the (voluntary) mouth. The flow of air touching the walls of the inner cavity of the mouth (palate, tongue, cheeks, uvula, nostrils) is recognized by its impacts there, and in order to know these impacts and their range of variation, babies, already conscious of somatic changes, engage themselves in their thorough study. Crying, for the baby, is the pursuit of this study.

It is well known that in a nursery babies just a few hours after birth join other babies in a crying chorus, giving the impression that they hear and imitate sounds from the start. Because nothing that has not already been mastered before birth is required for the baby to know from the inside what crying is, and because the auditory nerve (even as a bunched-up set of fibers) can still take to a baby's consciousness the impact of other babies crying, any baby who is not deaf will interpret at once that other people are doing what he can do, and he proves it by doing it.

But as soon as he gets involved in the vital new jobs mentioned above, he withdraws his consciousness from his hearing and leads a solitary life of his own. His chemical sense guides him to his source of food and he takes in what restores his chemical equilibrium. When this is achieved he stops eating and goes back to his work, he then looks to be asleep.

To be asleep is two things in one. For the outsider it is a withdrawal from the world; for the sleeper it is the return to what he knows best and has lived with most intimately.

Since we relate best to ourselves when asleep, and relate to others only when awake, here again there are many sources of confusion in trying to understand reality according to whether we stress the inner or the outer life.

Withdrawal into our own bag is taking ourselves to our own domain where knowledge and knowing reign. There we have only ourselves to contend with, and we know freedom because of the mastery we have of our functionings and because of our awareness of the dynamics of our energy.

Life *ex utero* contains so many unpredictable elements, so many unknown wills doing so many unknown things, that to wake up to it is justified only by our inability to continue a parasitic life.

2 Entering the World

Once we are linked to some people and discover that we can live by means of the covenant they offer us, we can consider waking up and displacing some of our attention from our soma and our functionings to that which the environment has to offer. In the next chapter we shall examine the baby's entrance into the environment in detail. Here we must still clarify two issues.

The first, a continuation of the above discussion of crying, is concerned with the expressions of crying that soon become communication, and the second is concerned with the other elements observable in babies at this stage: dreaming, smiling, the apparent expression of emotions.

Since only the baby knows when his system is short of energy or when a muscle is tensed or a tendon is twisted or when poison is at work in his tract, and since he can simultaneously use his breathing and his vocal cords, we find that the diversion of his attention from what he is working on (so as to master certain functionings) to the circumstances that demand casual but necessary attention, puts him into contact with the environment through the only open channel: his throat. Hence, once again, babies cry because they can and not to call for help. Cries express the awareness that one is forced to stop doing a job and cannot solve on one's own the problem with which one is faced.

That cries soon become a code between the learning baby and the environment should not obscure the fact that awareness is present in such crying too, and present in its own form and for its own purposes. Mothers, like their babies, know that there are many kinds of crying and that each has components indicating a special awareness of what the baby is engaged in.

The intensity, duration and pitch all convey that the child's self is either in contact with a pain of one kind or another, or is simply playing at crying in order to learn about noise production and how sounds can be modulated.

Crying, both when it is for the baby himself and when it is a form of communication, serves to alert babies to the possibilities of conscious investigation in the realm of sound, and we shall see to what good use young children put this opportunity in their apprenticeship to the task of talking and speaking.

The baby at this stage generally looks serene in sleep. Instrumental study of the state of his muscle tone shows a harmonious curve, as if the baby was imperturbable.

Because the sense organs have not yet been used to structure the mental energy that will soon activate them (this process will be examined in the next chapter), there are no images in the bag besides the body-image. The baby therefore does not dream.

The changes that are visible from outside on the skin of the baby are the outcome of the impact of energy changes on the muscle tone all over his body, these changes accompanying the development of the vital functionings now being studied and mastered. The muscles in the bag are capable of responding everywhere to a strong contraction anywhere. Weaker contractions affect fewer areas. When, for example, the flow of food in the tract is smooth, either no external change is visible or an elusive wave runs over the surface of the soma and forms around the lips and the cheeks what everyone calls a *smile*. A newly born baby can only "smile at the angels" for he is unaware of people in his neighborhood.

Any breakdown, small or large, in the new functionings can have considerable repercussions in the soma and is often accompanied by a great expenditure of energy through crying. Because the self is so close to its structure and its functionings, each baby is his own best physician. For example, the true meaning of the state of falling into a coma is the need for a total withdrawal to the self of all its energies so as to enable it to handle an aggression—in the form, say, of a poison or a foreign body. Babies in their very early days cure themselves and may go through diseases with no one suspecting the need for help.

It has often been said that newly born babies are born immune to a number of diseases, including the common cold. It seems more appropriate to say that the architect, the builder, the maintenance agent of the soma are together so close to the structure and the functionings that they have engendered that any disturbance is caught as soon as it starts and is taken care of at once. As consciousness moves towards other concerns, external help becomes necessary when illnesses occur. In the very young baby, health is the normal state, even when congenital defects exist. Most of these will become felt only when some functions emerge other than those essential for survival. Death in early childhood may express an inadequacy of the somatic construction, but many deformed and handicapped children do survive.

In the bag alongside the objectified energy there is free energy which the self can distribute, reserve or displace at will. When energy is mobilized but not objectified it gains a temporary form. We shall call *emotions* the "coagulation" of energy that the self recognizes within itself and that it can recuperate and reallocate.

Young babies already know this dynamic of energy within the bag and they use it very early in response or reaction to some aspects of the environment. They get involved for a very short time in some connection with people or with things but abruptly go back to their main "preoccupation." On the occasions of such involvement, they are caught up to the extent that they activate their relations to, and withdraw their energy from, the involvement. Indeed, if the enormous content of the environment were attractive to children of that age, it would exhaust all their energy, however much there is. Hence babies choose to "lend" rather than give attention, and they produce temporary inner impacts—emotions—that confirm to themselves that the dynamics of the energy in their bag is directed by their consciousness.

But this only covers those cases where the baby has a choice of being engaged in this or that. In other cases the temporary character of the connection is replaced by a more permanent one that may occasion an unnecessary reduction of the availability of energy and so traumatize the baby. In the chapter on love we shall study some of these cases.

2 Entering the World

Let us sum up the content of this chapter. We have followed closely the entry into our world of a being who knew the universe of his bag thoroughly, and we have found how he manages to relate creatively to new demands. The detailed descriptions of the new performances make us know babies as they need to be known—as learners and not as reflex mechanisms triggered by conditionings.

We have been able to gain an insight into sleep that makes much more sense than the notion that it serves the need to recuperate or that it is a mysterious process of wasting the time we could use for living. In particular, the capacity for solving problems, that accompanies some of our nights of sleep, is seen here as the outcome of the exercise of our freedom in a universe where the self reigns.

We have been able to understand why very young babies do not dream and why they smile or resort to crying.

The first few weeks are well used by each newly born baby as an adaptation to a world where so much happens that no chance of making sense of it is possible unless the baby directs his investigation and proceeds systematically.

3 Processing Energy

Parents say that their babies are "seeing" if they follow a moving finger or a moving light with their eyes. That they are "hearing" if they turn their head when dad or someone else snaps his fingers on one side and then the other. Parents dispute about their children's use of their sense organs because there is so often the appearance of perception but not its consistency.

We have already noticed in the previous chapter that newly born babies in hospital nurseries display the phenomenon of contagious crying, an aural phenomenon. They can also open their eyes, i.e. order their eyelids to separate and remain in that state for a while. These appearances militate in favor of a self active at the level of perception. But the baby knows better. When all his attention is required by studies which are essential for survival he will not engage in activities that are less vital at the time.

Pediatricians tell parents that for a few weeks after birth babies are insensitive to pain, and doctors perform operations like circumcision and the opening of the canals in the lachrymal glands without anesthetics. Their anatomy books tell them of a phenomenon called the "myelinization of the sensory nerves" which takes place a few weeks after birth and is presumably the point when babies become open to pain.

When myelinization occurs, which may be 4 to 6 weeks after birth, a sheath of fat is produced to surround each fiber and insulate it from the other fibers, rather like the wires in a telegraph cable. Doctors say that only after this has happened can sensations reach the centers that register impacts and cause pain to be felt.

This is not quite what closer observers can see. The facial expressions of babies operated upon without anesthetics during the first week after birth, and their crying, indicate that they note the aggression and "resent" it. But since they cope immediately with the somatic disturbance and are masters at coping with events at that level, they generally start the healing process at once and apply their consciousness so intensively to that job that little attention is left for unknown functions such as impressing the environment. If some complication results, say from infection or the clumsiness of the "surgeon," it is the deviation of energy from the known to the unknown that generates the traumatism and its expressions. Babies are at home with the soma that they made during the preceding months and know exactly what to do to cope with the events that make sense within their awareness. But, as in the rest of life, they will be lost when forced to consider what is transcendental to them at the moment and must then fall back upon guesswork as a response to the impact. If they are lucky their struggle will be victorious; if not, a scar may remain in the bag from then on.

Coping with what is incompatible with the existing functions costs a great deal more than coping with activities that are compatible and therefore leave no track. Throughout life the relation of the individual to his environment is harmonious if the encounter harmonizes with the ways of knowing available to him at the moment, and it is traumatic if the encounter is biased in favor of the environment that, in whatever way, is not taking into account what the individual is busy working at.

Since the myelinization of the sensory nerves takes a few days, the transformation of the self through the experience is gradual, and babies learn to place their consciousness upon the changes in the bag that result from the arrival of outside energy through the opened channels of their senses. One day, a few days after myelinization begins, they seem to be seeing and hearing, judged by outside observers devising their own tests. But for babies themselves the work of receiving the impact of the world started with their capacity to analyze a mental operation concomitant with the somatic transformation of each sensory nerve, active as a totality, into a set of nerve fibers active individually. The many thousands of nerve fibers, each associated at one end with a sense organ and at the other with a cell in the brain, are now capable of transforming impacts into inputs which the baby can notice because they bring additional energy to his soma.

The anatomical eye is made before birth. Seeing is no more the immediate result of opening one's eyes than digestion is the consequence of receiving food. There is much to learn in seeing and in the other sensory functions. It takes, in fact, years of subtle and continuous work to reach a high level of seeing, hearing and feeling because sensory functions relate each individual to a universe in flux that is therefore never completely knowable.

A baby knowing himself somatically opens up to a universe that philosophers (and perhaps all adults) conceive as a unity but which the baby meets as several universes according to the ways of knowing permitted by the structure and functions of the sense organs and by what consciousness can do with them.

The sensory functions are new functionings, new passages of energy, and new ways of knowing. Seeing, hearing and feeling lead to expanding universes within the bag that becomes more than the soma simply because of the displacement of consciousness (its movement from one area to another).

Because eyes, ears and skin offer consciousness different ways of receiving outside energy, new ways of knowing emerge which in turn make the self aware of itself in a multitude of different ways. This multiple self-awareness accounts for the uniqueness of the person just as the bag accounts for the physical uniqueness of the individual. What we do with ourselves in the total environment makes us into the persons we are. But what we are is never finished because our continuing encounter with other persons shows us ways of being that were open to us but which we have not actualized in our own lives, and through such encounters we can change.

Once the sensory organs come into active use, the individual self that made the soma engages more and more of itself in becoming aware of what can be done with the totality of the instruments available to it and with the instruments that these can be made to produce.

Let us take in turn the unfolding of those possibilities of the conscious instruments of the self that we call the sense organs.

Our eyes are made of parts that can be described anatomically, optically, mechanically and physiologically. All have their role in the function of seeing. The eyeballs can be moved in their sockets by small muscles attached to the bones and to the eyeball. These muscles are voluntary, linked to the brain by nerves that obey orders from the will. Babies have to learn to instruct these muscles to do what their self wills. At birth the only knowledge necessary to accomplish the movement of the eyeballs is that each muscle *in utero* has a *specific* muscle tone that can be altered in order to contract one muscle and relax another. Since muscles may pull in opposite directions, one aspect of this learning is to know how to activate one or more muscles and de-activate others for specific purposes. At birth the eye movements are left free to be educated by the self engaged in seeing and a few months are necessary to take this apprenticeship where the person wants. Some people concentrate on the dynamics of the orders given to these muscles and become circus or television stars because of the mastery they have achieved. Most children spend many hours over the years attempting to take the contact of their will with these muscles beyond the point they have reached so far to what they know is possible from having seen someone in their environment do it.

When we consider the relation of the self to an item in the bag that concerns the eyes we find at least this area of work for the consciousness.

The eyelids have been worked on before birth and most of us are born with the capacity to "open" our eyes. But once it is open to the world the optical system can become the object of attention when light reaches it. The eye, and therefore the self, receives a new input of energy. The baby responds to this impact when it is ready to.

We shall accept as a description of light the model of a discrete set of photons carrying their own energy and traveling from object to object through the ether at about 300,000 km. per second. Even if there are many difficult problems yet unresolved behind this model, it is the simplest for our purpose here.

Photons are energy particles. Associated with each of them there is a frequency that determines what we call its color. The amount of energy of each photon is very small compared with, say, that of an adult punching a training bag. We shall use an exact expression for this energy, hv, where v refers to the frequency (it is a whole number, in the trillions for visible light) and h is a universal constant, the same for all photons. The arithmetic product of h by v yields a result that is minute measured against the scale of everyday living. But if we consider huge numbers of photons the energy input may become considerable. Our eyes are indeed bombarded by a huge number of photons everyday.

The opening to the optical eye is made of a circular muscle that acts like a diaphragm in a camera, controlling the number of photons allowed in. For most of us its opening and closing is regulated by the amount of light reaching the eye. Such regulation is one of the automatisms organized by the self by delegating decisions to a special somatic compact, which in this case includes cells in the iris, sensory nerves, and motor nerves with their connections to the muscles of the pupil (so as to dilate or contract them to let more or less light reach the lens). This somatic piece (the lens) can let the light in, but it is also changeable in form so as to permit images to fall at the back of the eye exactly on the screen called the retina.

Accommodation, as this act of focusing is called, is both voluntary and automatic. The voluntary part makes it clear that seeing is a complex act. The sources of light are scattered all over space, and we need to interpret all the time the impacts of photons on the retina. In order to know the content of space, we have to relate consciously to the alterations of our soma resulting from the state of the iris, the state of the lens, the optic muscles that have been activated, the part of the retina that is struck by photons, and the individual and collective quality of the photons.

To see is nothing less than all this, and much more besides.

If we compare the naive view that most people hold, that eyes are made for seeing, against the enormous tasks we really have to engage in in order to use the eyes to learn to see, the place of consciousness becomes evident. Everyone of us as a baby needs to become aware of what the act of seeing involves so as to reach the most adequate automatization leaving us free for the other tasks involving seeing. For weeks each of us relates to light by knowing our eyes as optical instruments, allowing the energy of more and more photons to affect special areas of the brain and add to the somatic energy available.

Because the conscious act of seeing demands a particular mobilization of the self in which the self scrutinizes its own operations, we use here the word *look* as distinct from *seeing* to refer to the different role of the will in the act of seeing. Looking brings to seeing all the acquaintance of the self with the dynamics of the soma that mobilizes focusing, the reduction or expansion of the energy input, the duration of that portion of the input to be received, etc.—and that later includes much more, when the intellect and affectivity add their impacts, too.

After the education of looking, the first education in seeing concentrates on automatizing the awareness of the area of the retina that is being affected (its depth and expanse) and the presence or absence of photons of certain frequencies. For weeks the seeing eye becomes the object of the baby's attention and in the quietness of his crib he silently puts questions to his consciousness about the somatic variations that are being registered and their relation to others registered earlier. The energies of photons are recognizable because they bring with them external energy which is added to the system. The baby can know color as frequency long before he is able to label the source of the photons in the language of the environment.

A "film" of environmental light-changes can be assembled every day by the baby from material that he owns. When he is asleep the energy in the "film" is available to energize the cells of the retina under the control of a consciousness capable of perceiving identities, similarities, differences, durations, etc.—characteristics that are connected with the working instruments already available in his bag. This dialogue of the self in sleep is the process used to make the eye into an "image factory." The eye, instead of receiving photons now from outside, is made the judge (somatically) of the energy alterations that are produced by the will pouring energy into the cells to affect them in ways comparable with the effects caused by the input of photons from the environment. The self in the soma, the sleeping self to the observer, is very busy in the bag, educating the eye to evoke images at will (that is, to comprehend what it is seeing). It learns the parameters of this act so that it can explore at the same time, in the same act, the limits of reality and the freedom to alter reality—through activating for conformity or for a different end that it has chosen.

The act of evocation does two things. It makes the eye a tool of the self for producing images, for structuring mental energy according to the laws of sight and, therefore, through the new structures, transforming seeing; and, secondly, it generates a new set of labile structures in the bag, the images that the self knows as forms of energy that have been molded by the eye.

This dialogue of the self and the eyes goes on for years. It is non-verbal for a time and can remain so, but it is capable of transmutation by other conscious functionings, of which speech is one.

Seeing is also a way of knowing.

Because the awareness involved in seeing is the awareness of a set of cells subject to impacts of energy, knowing arrived at through the eye is necessarily synthetic. Babies cannot escape knowing that this kind of knowing is all-embracing and that the eye is the organ of panoramic evocation. In contrast, to know the details of a fresco requires a new dialogue with seeing which ends with a capacity to focus attention on the act of focusing optically—focusing being the process which makes a synthetic view compatible with an analytic view. We shall come to this process below.

Now, this extremely far-reaching structuration of mental functionings that starts so early in life takes place because, as babies, we acknowledge the reality of the content of the self and we recognize it in terms of energy and in terms of the qualities of the energy reachable through the dynamics of our soma.

Our soma is a complex knowing system, giving rise to other knowing systems which can become autonomous. In the case of seeing, once the visual images gain an existence of their own as semi-free energy in the bag, their life, mainly in the sleeping state, gains the autonomy to make dreams, and makes dreaming a new power of the self. In dreams the constraints of "reality" are no longer compulsory. New realities can be manufactured and the realm of the imagination is opened. Imagination becomes more and more a test of one's humanity because it is an expression of freedom.

The power to symbolize is also gained in this development, for once images gain their own existence the self knows both the reality of things and the reality of knowing about things. As the shift from one to the other becomes easier, better equipped, more frequent, the self finds for itself the endowment that comes from living with things, among things, but also from living next to them, outside them. That for some purposes evocation can replace actuality is the source of symbolism as power, and of symbols as the "things" of that parallel universe. From this power many others result during the journey through life. The example of sight shows us how much babies have to learn after they have assured survival outside the mother's womb for themselves.

We face two problems in studying the reality of babies in the world that they are opening themselves to. The first is to see what contributions to knowing oneself are brought by the various sense organs, and the second is to see how the line of evolution opens to the being who, though still physically a baby, has reached such levels of awareness. In this book the second problem can only be outlined, but the first will be investigated further with a detailed study of hearing.

While the eye receives minute pellets of energy that must accumulate to produce an impact beyond the threshold of somatic change, the ear receives packets of energy that need breaking down to be known. The eye is a synthesizer, the ear an analyzer. Each provides the baby with the corresponding mental instruments of synthesis and analysis.

The eardrum receiving the impact of an air mass in motion vibrates to its totality, the earbones then transfer the impulse to the liquid filling the inner ear, which funnels the energy into a smaller area and serves as a relay. A membrane made of independent hairs that can vibrate at different frequencies transfers a spectrum of frequencies to the brain through the auditory nerve.

Here again, as the myelinization of the auditory nerve goes on, consciousness perceives the various functionings of the parts, thereby allowing for concentration first of all on what it is necessary to hear.

The turning of one's head towards a source of sound, so that enough of the energy in the air can be bounced by the convolutions of the outer ear and canalized towards the drum, has to be experienced until it becomes automatic. The semi-circular canals serve as a gyroscope and associate a precise correspondence of the speed and angle of turning with the structures that oversee the other functions of the soma that are affected by movement.

Although the function of balancing the soma, delegated to these canals, is independent of the hearing process, it is not unrelated to the listening process. Listening, like looking in the case of sight, refers to the mobilization of the self in the ear so that the connection of the self to the source of sound is maximized. This connection involves the orientation of the head by using the upper two vertebrae to tilt and turn the head to achieve the best reception of the source—so long, that is, as this is not too loud, when the reverse position will be needed. Later on in his life every child plays at becoming dizzy and learns his capacity to spin safely.

Now, qualities that make noises recognizable, that allow the inner shift from noises to sounds and then to the various properties of sounds, must be accessible to the system used for recognitions which necessarily depend on analysis. The impacts on the eardrum could not be analyzed unless an analytic system were present, and this is indeed the way that awareness works on such impacts.

When, later in life, words are coined for the analyses already performed, the self knows what to designate as loud and soft by the total amount of energy it receives. For example, if the level of a sound diminishes, listening acts as an amplifier to enhance that level and lower the threshold of one's mobilization.

The recognition of continuity and intermittence is clearly a matter of analytic awareness. So is the frequency of succession of impacts, as long as they are distinguishable by the vibrating parts in the ear. On this variable, the self only knows the spectrum that the membrane—that is, the acoustic nerve ending in the ear—can register. In the case of musical sounds this spectrum is well defined; in the case of ordinary noises the analysis yields for each noise a (generally) distinctive composition. Because the analysis by the ear accomplishes this it becomes possible to distinguish thunder from a sanitation truck crushing cans, and both from the noise of a jet engine, etc. The presence of consciousness in the ear changes each impact into a distinctive awareness so that, for example, particular voices can be attributed to particular people even when one does not know the language used by these voices.

How else is sound used by the baby?

As newly born babies enter the world of sound, their somatic instrument—activated by the presence of consciousness encountering the aural impacts—also becomes activated at the other ends of the acoustic neurons, which are altered chemically and physically in a manner recognizable by the self (as all such alterations have been until now). As a result, the self knows now that the brain can experience changes because of added energy, and it learns to associate such changes with other components perceived by other sensors in the soma. The coordination of sensory perceptions is a further new component of the act of knowing. It remains a process of somatic alterations, but the alterations are the result of additional energy rather than of the dynamics of the energy already in the bag.

Like the eye, the ear can be an instrument of evocation. Sound images are energy of the self sent into the inner ear to be structured by the parts that can affect it selectively and held together as one chunk of energy.

As part of the self, images, either aural or visual, can be successively structured by different organs, and they end up holding the marks of all these various structurations. Our dreams witness to this complex nature of images where awareness, by focusing on them, activates the presence of the stamp given by the structuring sense.

Very soon after entering the world babies recognize direction of sounds as an attribute of the soma altered by impacts; slowly they attribute some sounds to some sources that are known through other procedures and perceptions. Awareness of these changed awarenesses links life to time. The simultaneous awareness of events in the bag (such as heartbeats, the flow of blood and lymph, breathing cycles) and also of perception provides a basis for the recognition of order in the impacts—the awareness that one impact is known to have occurred "after" another can be registered. Evocation relates "after" with "before" until both can be used to comprehend a sequence of somatic events.

Just as stressing the discontinuity of impacts on the ear provides an awareness of time, so stressing the simultaneity of impacts on the eye provides an awareness of space. Both time and space are awarenesses of states of the self in relation to the soma and what happens to it. These awarenesses could have been gotten *in utero*, and no doubt some people do get them there. But the probability that the self is alerted to the true characteristics of these awarenesses is greater when the sense organs are struck by unforeseen events not originating in the soma.

Babies learn these and other processes and learn to recognize the results from the very beginning of their entry into the world of perception. Perception gradually becomes more complex, but its existence and possibility is present from the start simply because it is awareness of the soma in relation to additional energy—that is, however, added to existing energy at work in systems already well known and working well.

The baby in the world can still control that part of his life which involves only himself, and he can filter impressions—which result from the random effect of the outside—so as to make sense of the world. Consciousness is present as much when assimilating impacts as when filtering them. The difference is that the first become part of one's bag while the others do not.

The displacement of consciousness (the sign that objectification does not exhaust the energy of the self) makes each baby capable of two operations which can take place simultaneously or separately. Every baby can *stress* and/or *ignore* any item in his bag by simply placing and/or withdrawing his consciousness from it.

Stressing *and* ignoring at will makes each baby capable of *abstraction*, for abstraction only means the action of leaving out everything except that which one wants to retain.

Of course, stressing and ignoring have been at work already in the embryo, but now we can gain some new insights into the life of the baby by calling in the process. By activating any component of the sound that reaches one's ear, by associating the effect of stressing this component on various activities in the bag, the self can become aware, in their simultaneity, of new functionings. The baby therefore gives himself new powers that open new universes of experience to him.

In particular he can now acknowledge the simultaneity of the synthetic and analytic approaches to everything that has an impact on him, as well as to his evocations. He can listen to the totality of a sound and to any element of it he focuses on and be aware of both simultaneously. He can look at a field of vision and focus on a detail and be aware of both simultaneously.

As a result of his ability to stress and ignore items in his experience, he is guided by the sights or sounds or smells or tastes that he has stressed and made himself familiar with and he structures his acquaintance with the environment in relation to these choices.

For example, a baby's consciousness has been engaged from birth, through his need to eat, with his mouth and he has made it an instrument for knowing. Until other functionings begin to compete with it and are preferred for some reason, the baby continues to use it when he wants to know the characteristics of some object. As we know, for some months babies take to their mouth any objects that they want to know intimately.

The skin, too, is such a guide. Because the skin is vulnerable to pressures, variations of temperature, and impacts which are felt as pleasant, smooth, rough, prickly, etc., it becomes an instrument for knowing both oneself and the environment. There is a universe that the sensors of the skin can explore. Because a map of the skin's experiences can be made in the brain through simultaneously becoming aware of what happens to the skin and what happens at the other end of the nerve fibers in that portion of the brain called the hemispheres, there is a spectrum of nerve alterations in the bag that inform the self of what is happening to the skin in its contact with the outside world.

Every baby has to learn to interpret any impact upon his skin in terms of his body-image. The outside surface of the bag is kept under continuous surveillance by his consciousness placed in some brain cells whose states have been catalogued to indicate what is happening to the skin. (The advantages of surveying just a portion of the brain for energy changes over surveying the entire surface of the bag are so obvious that the very young baby reaches the same conclusion.) He uses this instrument of surveillance to respond to changes on the surface of his bag by directly associating changes within the surveying cells to a set of instructions passed to other parts of the brain, thereby triggering changes in the tone of selected muscles, which in turn produce actions related to the initial changes on the skin. It all looks as if the brain is in command, when in truth it operates only as a delegate of the self—that acts selectively on minute alterations of the energy levels in the cells of the brain so that these alterations extend themselves through the neurons to their extremities on the inner surface of the skin.

This period of life can most appropriately be called "the education of the hemispheres" since this compact organization in the soma learns how to hold the energy brought from the outside through the sense organs, bringing the awareness of which cells have been affected and to what extent.

3 Processing Energy

Only consciousness is capable of doing the many jobs that have to be done by the baby to cope with the environment. Only consciousness can delegate to part of itself another part that serves to inform it of any alteration in the first, and which can link this alteration to any other that it wills. It can do it because of the knowledge consciousness, whether free or objectified, has of itself.

The baby at this stage remains in close contact with the quanta of energy received through the eyes, the packets of energy received by the ear, and the impacts received upon the skin (including the tongue and the nostrils), and notices what happens to some cells in the hemispheres because of these various impacts. The knowledge of the soma by the self is such that (through all the feedback mechanisms it has established) it can maintain contact with the neurons that have been affected by the photons reaching the retina, or the vibrations of the hairs in the inner ear, or the nerve endings (or papilla) on the surface of the bag (including the inner mouth and tongue and the walls of the inner nose).

Such intimacy makes the self capable, if the need arises one day, of re-educating parts of the brain, which the self knows to have remained unaffected, to take on functions that had been associated with cells no longer available (because of a wound or a disease).

The way of learning to see, hear and feel that we have discussed is still very close to the functionings of the soma. Babies who have completed these studies are probably about seven to eight weeks old.

To sum up this chapter, we have seen how powerful an instrument of study has been the presence of consciousness from the start. It has permitted us, in particular, to give the brain its true place in our life and to avoid being stood against the wall of either materialism or metaphysics.

Consciousness can relate to itself, and since it is present in every cell and in every amount of energy in the soma, it knows when additional energy is brought to the soma. It can follow the destiny of these quanta and integrate them, and at the same time it knows their source, at least from the moment they enter the sense organs.

Taking note of these phenomena as they happen to the soma is the essential work of babies at this age.

Our discussion in terms of awareness shows us a knowledgeable baby seriously engaged in knowing the truth and, although working in a way not reachable by outsiders, doing the job very well.

When the baby's acquaintance with the energy taken in through the senses is secured, new jobs can be entered upon. Some of these will be studied in the next chapters.

4 The Temporal Hierarchies

Since there is so much to learn about the world in which we are born, and since in the realm we are considering the baby must do his own learning, can we find a rationale for a baby choosing to be involved in one activity rather than any other?

If before entering into any activity a baby needs to know which instruments are required, he must have access to this knowledge, a *sine qua non* condition quite distinct from employing them in the new activity. There are two ways he can use to attain this knowledge. One is a chance awareness. The other is to attempt to extend the instruments he is already using, either by combining them or by deliberately applying them to an activity he perceives as relating to these instruments. In every life there are a vast number of instances of each opportunity. A new involvement by a baby can guide an observer towards finding the path that has been selected and can suggest the reasons why.

For example: it is not necessary to listen to oneself crying, but it is possible and, if a baby does it, his ear can find in the sounds he hears an involvement that may strike him as worth pursuing. Crying is conscious and since hearing has become the focus of attention, a bridge can be established between the capacity to make noises and the capacity to recognize them. Because his capacity to make noises is voluntary, a baby may easily give himself the task of establishing in the ear a new set of criteria concerning sounds to replace the set he already owns.

Knowledge of the sounds he produces is accessible to him because this consciousness dwells in the muscles of his chest, the walls of his lungs, the vocal cords, the muscles of his mouth; indeed, to say that the emission of sounds is voluntary means just that. Once this knowledge is coupled with a study (through listening) of their impact on the eardrum, a new awareness is open and his brain can now act as a register of the willed sounds for recognition by the ear, paralleling or replacing the recognition that operates through the simultaneous awareness of muscle tone changes in a number of places—an awareness already active through prenatal practice.

Once this set of criteria is established it can serve as a monitor of all utterances—and indeed all speakers use it all the time, forgetting the voluntary part which is now automatic, and depending on the alertness of their hearing and listening to check spontaneously the correctness and adequacy of their spoken words.

Before a baby engages in the task of speaking he has to have solved problems like the above, even though he cannot suspect that it plays any role in the apprenticeship to a language of which he as yet knows nothing.

Having been born capable of acting on the muscle tone of all his energized muscles and finding his hands endowed with units (called fingers) that he can activate separately, not to mention his awareness of other muscles in his wrists and his forearms, the baby may by chance enter into the dialogue of contracting and relaxing some of these muscles and noting the effect. Once awareness has been brought to the realization of such changes, a universe suddenly opens up that takes the baby—through exercises devised by himself—to the knowledge that his hands are instruments for grasping objects, for turning them, for throwing them, for acting upon materials in a number of ways. For many days this awareness provides the baby with endless opportunities to transform into instruments what he is learning through games.

Noticing that while on his back he can affect the muscle tone of his lower back and thighs and thereby obtain the result of lifting his legs, he becomes an expert at bringing his feet near his face or shoulder—or even at putting his big toe into his mouth.

This mastery of what is required in order to act upon the legs permits him to form a right angle between them and his thorax and abdomen. Imagine a baby who can grasp the railings of his crib, and hold fast to them, and who also can fold his legs up until a right angle is formed: he requires to expend only a small amount of additional energy to find that the rotundity of his buttocks will transform this right angle into another right angle, this time with the body vertical and the legs and thighs lying on the crib. He will have taught himself to sit and to sit up.

This is something, it is worth pointing out, he must necessarily teach himself. Even if by chance people have already lent him their fingers to grasp and have lifted his body vertically, while he is still in his crib, although he looks as if he is sitting the experience will not teach him how to sit. He may learn from it that he is able to hold his body vertically once left to his own devices, but in order for him to know how to sit a conscious knowledge is needed of how to use somatic energy to displace the center of gravity from its position when one is on one's back to the position it must take in sitting.

To go back to other prior steps, displacing one's center of gravity cannot be done without using the hands to hold on to something and putting them in a place that is compatible with the rotation required. Hence the study of how to place the thumb against the fingers, the study of holding, of holding on, of pulling, all of which means reaching the knowledge of which muscle tone one has to vary and by how much (one varies, actually, the muscle tone), is all a prerequisite of a particular activity that requires these items and must be mastered before a baby can sit up.

This further example of what we shall call a *temporal hierarchy* makes clear that one's consciousness is the key to success in any activity and that without it there is no attempt to entertain such activities nor any chance of success. Parents cannot teach their children any skills that demand a number of prior activities that the parents do not know about. Parents may see that if they do certain things they help their child *to sit*, but they do not help him to *learn to sit*. This he alone can manage, precisely because he alone can know the actual transformations of muscular energy required to reach a particular state.

Much earlier in his life a child has had to learn how to put his thumb in his mouth. This trivial exercise is full of traps and is only achieved because consciousness is guided by the body-image, which tells the contracted arm that it is being placed at the proper angle and in the proper place to achieve the entry of the extended thumb in the invisible mouth. Trials and errors are needed to solve this problem, as many facial scratches testify to.

Thumb sucking is not something that a baby is taught from the outside; it is something he teaches himself through his consciousness by developing the appropriate skills over a period of time. But why should a baby want to suck his thumb?

He will not want to before he can do it (even if it occurs *in utero*, as is reported in some cases), but the motivation cannot be solely in this capacity. He could perhaps put his fingers in his nose, or ear, or even his eyes; but he does not do these things. Is it not possible that every baby knows that frictioning his gums reduces the pain caused by the teeth pushing at and breaking through the cartilage of the gums?

The knowledge that relief can be obtained in this way is certainly available to the baby. No one teaches us to press against any part of our body to relieve a neuralgia. The action is such a spontaneous response, known from our intimacy with our soma, that in circumstances such as a rapid descent of a plane, passengers put their fingers in their ears although the action is useless.

That teeth are growing in the gums, and that relief of pain can be obtained by massaging them, could well be the motivation for so many babies in all cultures discovering how to insert their thumb in their mouth. If this is done for many months, who can expect that the habit can be easily broken?

Living is the consumption of public time.* The inner equivalent of this process can be found in the temporally stratified hierarchies of awarenesses.

Once these awarenesses are present they can be integrated with subsequent awarenesses. Every baby knows that he is changing time into experience and that this experience can have a form, an objectification, resulting from the energy mobilized for some new function.

Before a baby knew how to sit, he had many functionings at his disposal that he needed in his attempt to learn to sit. Then, by learning to sit, he added an *integrative schema* to his awareness, and while all the functionings required are still available to him as before, the act of sitting has brought them into a relationship that gains an existence of its own and can be practiced *per se*.

---

* The time generated by the rotation of the Earth around the sun and around itself.

So it is when a baby learns to crawl, learns to stand and learns to walk. None of these future achievements is the direct consequence of the existing components. A new schema, as if it were falling upon the baby from the future, makes him consciously reorganize the appropriate competences to display now what was not there before.

Integration is the process by which the future affects that which already exists. Every baby who finds himself doing one new thing after the other, creating new constellations of existing behaviors for new ends, cannot fail to know himself as living in the future, as meeting the unknown, the unforeseen.

Again, the process is entirely an inner one. Only when a baby knows how to perform certain acts can he find that a similar act is being performed by others—similar, not the same, for the action he sees uses another soma and is perceived from outside, while he knows his own action from inside.*

There is no difference due to age in the way we distinguish those perceptions which arise from the outside from those coming from the inside. We have to grant to babies that they know what is accessible to the instruments clearly at work at each stage, and we need not shift to mysterious notions such as experience and maturity when only awareness is at stake. The concept of temporal hierarchies speaks of the necessity for some

---

* When we hear our recorded voice for the first time we either fail to recognize it or are amazed at its characteristics. The reason is that we have a resonance chamber in our mouth and, as we speak, the sounds reflect on the walls and are transmitted by the bones of our skull, adding a number of perceptible components within the bag that are not present when the eardrum alone is struck. Our voice is far less odd if we hear it on video, for sight convinces us that it is ours.

awareness, some functioning, or some organ to serve as an instrument to generate further awarenesses or even new functionings (corresponding perhaps to some man-made "organ" such as speech). Change or development in the self needs nothing more.

The presence of consciousness in a temporal hierarchy leads usually to three forms, depending on whether: (1) consciousness is entering knowingly into a dialogue with the self as it is now, or (2) consciousness is consciously dwelling in newly mastered functions, or (3) consciousness is using the totality of the automatic functions (each requiring only that modicum of energy to maintain it in a state of adequate service and to inform the self). This trinity of the states of consciousness—the yesterday, the today and the tomorrow of the self—is ours all though our conscious life and is available to everybody. It is the testimony that the individual is a person and can transform himself to take care of what comes.

Because babies know this as the reality of life, they display, as a natural component of their outlook, an attitude that can be called the *suspended judgment attitude*, which, when it is lost through faulty education, seems a precious power to have had.

Since the world is full of unknowns, how could a knowing self do anything other than suspend judgment?

But what a tremendous power it is to leave to tomorrow the final verdict on what has been lived today!

As babies and young children we know how to do this "naturally," and it allows us to develop the attitudes required by the learning we engage in. Although the process is clearest in the study of the speech of babies it is not special to that area. Its validity is the result of the temporal nature of life, because we need time to objectify, to become aware of details, to practice. Moreover, so long as this quality of life is known to the self, suspension of judgment will be the attitude taken by the self when engaged in any activity. The proof of this can be found in the absence of a feeling of failure in a child engaged in any true learning, as in a genuine involvement in a game suited to his age. There is no expectation of doing better than one did, but rather the dwelling on what to do next so that inadequate functionings become more adequate to the challenge.

Another aspect of temporal hierarchies can be found in the balanced oscillation between synthetic and analytic functionings, both of which are always possible although not necessarily simultaneous.

We already saw how this dual engagement of consciousness works in the case of seeing and hearing. Available to all babies, it seems a much more effective approach to learning than the trial-and-error technique occasionally used. Truly it is hard to conceive that the very complex achievements demanded of the very young could result from any blind technique able, like trial-and-error, to reach only atoms of knowledge. Instead, babies need to develop the tools of understanding that are capable of holding vast masses of data received simultaneously and to interpret rapidly the significance of particular elements. The alternating use of synthesis and analysis is such a tool.

For instance, learning to sit or to crawl, or, earlier still, learning to "spin round one's navel," all involve the synthesis of impulses directed to a large number of muscles, which together end up as a single activity that can be judged for adequacy and selectively altered so as to satisfy a vigilant self whose precise feedback mechanisms are at work in the sensors of the units involved. If this were not so, to repeat a phrase used earlier, we would be facing continuous miracles.

Standing offers another example. Every baby who can sit and can use his arms to lift himself up can also feel his legs and feel how his weight affects his skeleton. He is at once informed whether the stage of calcification, which goes on under the guidance of the middle brain (itself inhabited by the remnants of consciousness that control its functioning and inform higher layers of the brain of what is happening), is sufficient to provide, along with the muscles, the support to counteract gravity.

This information is vital to the young child learning to stand and can reach his consciousness directly (if his self is in contact with the nerve center, to which delegation of controls was given) or indirectly (if the test of attempting to stand is followed by a signal that the weight is too much for the strength of the supporting parts of the soma all working together).

The fact that some children do stand in spite of the signal telling them that the calcification is insufficient, ending up with bow legs instead of straight legs, can be counted as a sign of a freedom of choice at this level. A choice at one point in life may

4 The Temporal Hierarchies

have consequences that can become traumatic at another level of awareness of the soma—at adolescence, for example.

There are children who crawl before standing or walking, and others who don't. Since this particular learning cannot be inspired by the imitation of the all-powerful adults around, we can study crawling in its simultaneous use of synthesis and analysis to provide a temporary solution to the challenge of locomotion by a self who has discovered how to use what is available to him. (Whether locomotion is motivated by the desire to reach something or not is irrelevant here, for we want to know what babies do and how, rather than why.)

To be able to crawl a baby must know the following, all at the same time: that his skin is in contact with a supporting surface which cancels his weight *and* that his contact with this surface can be altered selectively by affecting the tone of specific muscles *and* that by pressing on the surface with some parts of himself while lifting some other parts a thrust ahead results *and* that this can be repeated, stopped or altered in a number of ways.

It takes time to learn to crawl, but once learned it can be perfected and taken to truly amazing levels of efficiency for a locomotive skill that will soon be replaced by a very different one.

It is interesting to see babies who have learned to walk still use crawling to reach some ends when they can rely more definitely on this form of locomotion than on walking. If all this were "instinctual," as naive observers say, how could this particular choice of behavior be understood? In fact no learning in human babies can be instinctual because awareness provides the data, and there is always judgment synthesizing the perception of a challenge and the knowledge of the self's capabilities at all levels where awareness has been at work, from conception onwards.

When we think of the complexities of the universe and the short time it takes babies to learn so much, we have to grant to each baby an arsenal of ways of knowing in keeping with the number and diversity of the challenges it confronts.

The caution shown by babies when taking the first steps in any learning is the sign that the knowing self is meeting the unknown, *not* the sign of a clumsy system suddenly attempting to shift its functionings through accommodation to new stimuli. Babies seize a challenge with all that is available to them and express their grasp by a test to know if the intuition is correct. As soon as a test is successful a bolder attempt is made, still in accordance with the intuition. If this is confirmed a swift displacement of consciousness moves the lighting on the challenge and provides analytic, sure knowledge that creates the integrative behavior that alters the challenge into part of the system, and alters the system through the integration of the former challenge.

Intuition is the only way of knowing the unknown through what can be grasped of it while respecting all that cannot be reached analytically at the time. Intuition, as part of the conscious self, is known as a way of knowing among others, a necessary approach when the unknown is experienced. That it is replaced at other moments on other occasions by other ways of knowing does not make it invalid; it only speaks of the discriminating self using adequate approaches according to its perception of the actual situation confronting it.

Without intuition no one could do more than respond timidly to discrete stimuli; with it, bolder, encompassing steps are in order.

We have assumed the success of the first steps, but if there are problems, the suspended-judgment mechanisms make the baby stop in his tracks and consider whether he will postpone any further movement in the area of his present concern or attempt alternative solutions. All parents know examples of such manifestations of the "intelligence" of their child in his pre-verbal stages. For instance, the discovery by a child that a rail can be used to take some of the weight of his body if he holds on to it may provide him with the opportunity of preparing for walking—that is, for using certain muscles of the legs and thighs for certain ends.

Once a child has enough acquaintance with the balance required to stand without support, he may give himself a new challenge and contract some muscles of only one leg, thus generating an opportunity to fall. If after the contraction the baby quickly tries to restore his balance with the same leg, he will most likely end up with his two legs no longer side by side. If he does restore the equilibrium he will have discovered that balanced standing can be accommodated to a number of different angles of the thigh-leg systems. A repetition of the exercise may result in a new phenomenon, the fact that his body has been successfully displaced from here to there—and the awareness of walking is born.

Some children may take weeks between their first step and their first sequence of steps. This depends on the kind of consciousness that accompanies the discovery of how to restore balance after a failure in the act of walking. If no emotion intervenes there may be no postponement of the progression from one to more steps, but only the baby knows his state, only he knows what he is focusing upon in all these solitary exercises involving the self as free energy and the self as soma.

Temporal hierarchies are safe instruments for the understanding of babies' adventures in their world. They allow us to avoid believing in either the rigid sequencing or the random happening of their activity, and make us look at what actual particular situations demand of learners. It so happens that we all, or almost all, end up doing mostly the same things in almost the same way. But this is only the appearance, and even if we end up at the same place it does not mean we have followed the same route.

The reality of each of us does not matter to anybody except to each of us, and it is useless to try to reach the "reality of all" or to replace individual realities by an overall, empty concept not true of anyone.

4 The Temporal Hierarchies

Since each of us lives in time and the time of one's life belongs to each of us to be spent deliberately for the purpose of being who we can be, with our true endowments in our given environment, we can only follow our own path to obtain a conscious balance and integration of the actual experiencing which was and is ours. What we leave out and what we integrate is, seen from outside or from inside, descriptive of an actual life and permits the great variety that we are, at birth and forever.

Variety testifies to the options that are open, to be taken or not, and the temporal edifice of each life makes us all different from each other in spite of the ease with which one person can be spatially identified with another. Looked at from outside, people are alike; looked at from inside, from the temporal viewpoint, everyone is different. Indeed we are all very different, even if twins.

By selecting temporal hierarchies rather than structures as our instrument of description, we have made it possible to have a language that maintains the truth of variety and of singularity without at the same time eliminating a possibility of mutual assimilation. We all have to observe temporal hierarchies to end up able to do comparable things, but we never end up reproducing the same structure, for the structures are the objectification of sequences in time and these sequences respect only one demand: that in order to function freely and adequately what is integrated must exist before it can be integrated.

Memory is another name for awareness at work within temporal hierarchies. Our memory can be an automatic functioning that neither needs recalling nor is required to be recalled; there need only be a sense that the functioning is part of the whole and responds to selective calls.

It can also be a chain of evocations, some directly accessible, some accessible only when some others have been activated, each recognized as belonging singularly to oneself. It can also be certain deliberate mobilizations of energy for the various individual purposes that both life in the world and the inner life demand.

To know what memory is involves not only knowing the contents of one's own memory, but also being aware of a panorama of consciously lived experience criss-crossed with the tracks made by consciousness sometimes returning to previous impressions, recognizing them, and knowing that it recognized them.

The memory of babies does not differ essentially from that of adults, only the "material" that corresponds to the involvement of awareness does. Children have relatively as much to remember as adults, and recall and recognition are of a kind all through life. But the passage of time means that what has been at one stage consciously investigated subsequently becomes instrumental, most of it becoming automatic, so that an adult's memory has deeper layers of temporal hierarchies which, though functioning, are inaccessible.

We can take another perspective. Looking at a life of any length at a particular moment, it shows three temporal layers: the lived, the one being lived now, and the one to come. Each layer exists at *any* moment, so the time traversed in looking back at the lived will pass through the being-lived and some of that which is to come. Because they are capable of such assimilation the three layers must have essentially the same attributes. What carries us from "what was not" to "what is" must be one thing, the self, which makes consciousness and the unconscious one, consciousness and the transcendental one.

To see time in one's life as the future descending to become first the present and then the past is as valid as, and perhaps more adequate than, the notion of a past that defines each of us. To be in time is also to let time do its work and to see oneself as never finished, never complete, always involved in meeting what has not yet had form in one's own life.

We all have to go through our own experiences and no one can live on our behalf even when we live by proxy. The length of one's life does not take away this. Each of us has to learn what has to be part of himself, and by learning, his self is changed. We cannot save time by being instructed, but perhaps we can save time by recognizing and utilizing more effectively the various roles of the various powers of our self made evident in our various learnings.

There are awarenesses within the self that make us perceive ourselves as changing, or make us perceive in our self the dynamics of change. To live in time is to acknowledge that transformations are the true fabric of our being; that without them we would be annihilated.

Babies as well as adults need to know which transformations make living possible; indeed all persons who survive know them and use them. Babies know that they never see the world except in flux. They do not choose to be lifted and moved around, and the classes of impressions they have of every object and every person are the only truth they know.

It is because of our capacity to stress and to ignore, that recognition is possible in a world in flux. Only in the mind do classes gain a stability. Babies see their parents change clothes, appearance, smell, and so on; they see people come close and disappear, changing appearance in so many ways, and this is their true world. It would be chaos if the power of recognition that permits us to ignore elements that can distract, and to stress others that generate permanences, was not also the way of knowing of children.

Recognition has a link with memory, although in ordinary usage memory is more the power to retain or to recall, the capacity to maintain with fidelity the attributes of permanent objects. Recognition is memory at work in reality, that is adapting itself to the reality of objects which, rather than being defined once and for all, are classes of impressions that permit some variation in them at the same time as they permit the formation of a chain of equivalences linking them.

"Mother" is a set of impressions that allow her to lead her life in the world—having her bath, dressing up to go out, smelling of soap or perfume or sweat or frying oil, her hair down or up, being so near that only a small bit of her face is visible, or in the next room, or in her car moving away. Which impression is mother? All and none. No unique image can be evoked and labeled mother.

Instead, the normal way of knowing is used, sometimes recognizing her by some smell, some other times by her voice, some other times by her smile or by her face. So long as the dominant impression evokes the class, mother will be known, and all the potential associations with her will be available.

It is therefore not the knowledge of himself as an object among objects that makes a baby reach his identity, but the acceptance of the myriads of impressions and the use of some temporal principle of assimilating some of them into cohesive classes that puts him safely into the reality that we are all in.

These open classes of impressions lend strength to the suspended-judgment attitude, for the baby knows that he does not rule the world around him and that for each class there may be new elements springing from nowhere which will claim a place in it. Mother may have a new dress on, or be very ill for the first time; an unknown visitor with the same name as the baby's may come to his home; father may come back from a journey having grown a beard.

Babies are at peace with change simply because they perceive it as the basis of reality. They know that what they see at a distance will look different when they move towards it or when it moves towards them. Hence they are not dismayed to see people disappear at the end of a road, and they do not look for an object that disappears unless they relate to it and want to have it again, as may happen with toys lost in their cribs. Young children do not mind accepting the appearance that the moon walks with them as they walk *and* also walks with someone else walking in the opposite direction—which is, indeed, the real set of impressions even if it is not an acceptable result in a logical system free of contradiction.

The moon indeed moves with me when I walk in opposite directions. If I trust my perceptions, I must grant this property to the moon. After all, I did not make the world; I only meet it as it is. When later I make separate categories that I acknowledge to be mutually exclusive and find data that tell me that illusions exist and that I must give more credence to one system than to another, I shall merely separate the two phenomena in my mind.

For me, as for Galileo, "e pur si muove." The moon does march on, even if it is indifferent to what I do on Earth.

We must also place in the context of temporal hierarchies the relationship of the self to its own awareness. As the self goes on using time to live and to experience and to generate forms and awarenesses, everything touched by its awareness is susceptible to study, to being known more deeply, to being kept in mind for years, even though it is not in focus all the time. A baby's self can and does notice that recognizable impressions exist, and he groups them. One impression can be recalled and another be actual, both being known for what they are. Later, both will be capable of being recalled alone or with another actual impression. This capacity provides both an instrument called *association* (which seems to be part of the functioning of memory) and a chance for a new awareness of *virtual activity and learning*. The latter only requires noticing that, in one's bag, imagery, emotions and impressions are part of the dynamics of the energy of the self, and the new awareness gives these elements a status equal to the one it already gives to the added energy obtainable from the outside.

Because each baby can be touched by the inner dynamics of his self he is aware of his awareness and can make use of it. He does not learn this from anybody, and what he does with it is entirely his own. Virtual learning will be favored or not by him according to the opportunities offered by other impressions from the world. One child will prefer to pursue a line of learning because he finds that if he does the learning virtually he is closest to it and thus avoids distractions; another finds that is fun to do the same in actuality, with the participation of others, but not allowing them to interfere.

There are a few children who learn to speak without ever uttering a word until they can speak fluently; games in which the players take turns provide them with an alternation of actual and virtual participation; solving mathematical problems or planning the architecture of a building are totally virtual activities.

At all stages, except perhaps the embryonic, we can notice that the surplus free energy of the self can be used by the self to do what it senses is compatible with its existing states, whether these are objectified or not. When an eight or nine month old baby discovers that he can simultaneously use his actions and his imagery, he brings them together in actual games of make-believe. For instance, he feeds his mother virtually, actually making all the gestures but with an imaginary spoon and an imaginary bowl of food. Through this he tells his environment that the actual and virtual universes have been integrated and that he can move in this new universe freely, doing what is compatible with it, stressing and ignoring in turn whichever element he chooses. From then on what he does with the integrated universe is his choice, and in order to know what this is, outsiders must learn new ways of looking at children.

To sum up this chapter, we can say that the perspective of the temporal hierarchies is perhaps one of the most versatile instruments that psychologists will benefit from using in order to really understand children and grant to them what is theirs.

Although babies are small, their discrimination at the level of their engaged consciousness does not leave anything to be desired compared with that of older people. Size is no attribute of maturity. In employing the perspective of temporal hierarchies, we give ourselves a chance of seeing wisdom at work on elements other than family, social and business concerns. Wisdom is displayed by babies at every stage of their dialogues with their successive universes because wisdom is nothing other than the candid recognition of what one is able to do and what one is permitted to do. It seems therefore that wisdom may be found in later years if it has at all ages been enhanced by a sense of realism in connection with whatever one is involved in.

4 The Temporal Hierarchies

It is no harder to be wise in society than it is to use discrimination to cope with teething by putting one's thumb in one's mouth, or to use discrimination in following the inner dynamics of emotions and not let them dissipate the self's energy in fits. Each of us is given opportunities to know himself engaged in knowing himself in the world, and hence knowing himself as part of the world. Each opportunity must be taken here and now and not be postponed to later years.

Temporal hierarchies are layers of life, no one better than another, no one more precious than another, but simply one after the other, each giving to a preceding one a position of foundation for others and each giving to a subsequent one a position of integration of others. All must be taken care of consciously and conscientiously in order to bring us health now and later. To this process we have been fitted as human beings.

5 Talking

As an instrument for understanding babies one question has been used a number of times, "What can they do on their own without help from others?" In this chapter we are going to study in detail one activity of all babies and see what progress this way of working yields.

We have already observed in the studies in the fields of sight and hearing made in Chapter 3 that the awareness that there is an inner movement, as well as a movement from the outside world to the self, must have been noticed quite early in mankind's evolution because all languages distinguish with separate words these two relationships of the self and the environment. To *look*, as we noted, is to mobilize the self in the eyes so as to become aware of the bombardment of the retina by photons, this awareness resulting in the self *seeing*. To *listen* is to mobilize the self in the ears so as to be able to *hear* what reaches the drum. There are two different verbs because there are two distinguishable awarenesses in these fields, and the differences serve as pointers for the study of learning.

We also have two words in the field of language: *talking* and *speaking*. They are today *almost* totally overlapping in meaning, but we shall distinguish them completely, as was possible in the fields of sight and hearing, and restrict their meaning here to a similar sort of separation: talking joins looking and listening, to express the subject's activities, those he can do on his own, and speaking joins seeing and hearing, to take account of what the world has to bring to the self (the social world in the case of language, as against the natural, Earth world for sound and the cosmic world for light).

Two chapters are devoted to this total activity to indicate the social significance of the area, although there is at least as much study to do in order to know as explicitly what can be known in the other areas we have been considering.

A big difference between the way the eyes and the ears relate to the impacts they have been built to receive is that the eyes must be turned towards the source of photons, otherwise nothing happens, while sounds can go round obstacles to make the eardrums receive their impact. It is only to increase or decrease the amount of energy reaching the eardrum that one will turn one's head. Sounds force attention while photons do not.

When a baby makes sounds in his crib he will be able to hear them if he wills it, and if his ear and acoustic nerve function properly. As soon as he acknowledges that it is he who is making the sounds that he hears, he has at his disposal two sources of information, his throat and his ear, to investigate the world of his own utterances. This chapter is devoted to a summary of what this investigation leads to. In the course of our discussion we may take up again some matters touched upon earlier, but here the study will be systematic.

Simply because a baby, whose sensory nerves have become selective conductors of impulses, can relate what he hears to what he does, he has the necessary equipment to study his sound production machinery and make it do what he wants.

From his *in utero* experience he knows how to affect the muscle tone of every muscle involved in phonation. This knowledge is conscious, and therefore phonation is a field he can reach in as much detail as he needs. Hence he can study separately or in conjunction the parts played by an air flow impinging upon the various components of the chamber that a closed mouth represents.

He can slow down the air flow by acting upon his lungs and his chest. He can open his larynx by separating the lips of the vocal cords, or bring them together as close as possible and see what the impact of the energy given by the air travelling at different speeds does to their vibrating ends (which he knows directly because they are part of his conscious soma).

By simply displacing his attention to other parts of the chamber he can know how the dynamics of the air affects them, and learn how variations in the muscle tone of his cheeks, palate, tongue and lips, in various combinations, affect the air flow. Every baby a few weeks old does this during those hours of crying that no adult any longer understands. This necessary knowledge in terms of muscle tone gives the muscles the quality of being instruments for knowing because awareness of a set of impacts informs the self what is happening in the chamber.

The six- or seven-week-old baby is actively taking note of what happens to the flow of air when he voluntarily changes the shape of his outer mouth by acting deliberately on the muscle tone of the various fibers in his lips. If he coordinates the amount of energy given to the flow of air, the shape of the lips, and the rest of the parts required for phonation, a somatic knowledge of what is being achieved results. It will be sufficient to instruct the same muscles in the same way to feel that the soma is in the same state. Learning at this level is a move towards the mastery of the dynamics involved so that the self is certain it can produce a synthesis of lips, air flow, etc., that confirms the conscious somatic project.

With knowledge extending over a set of such somatic syntheses a baby is equipped to move towards another synthesis, provided only that he can hear.

Observation of babies a few weeks old may not reveal deafness since the inner awareness of somatic states, our subject so far, is accessible to the baby via the way of knowing that resides in the awareness of muscle tone. Indeed, that deaf people can learn to utter what they do not hear guarantees that this way of knowing is open to every child who can "read" the energy variations as they appear in the organs of phonation through the dynamics of muscle tone.

Progress in understanding some other language impediments may arise from a closer look at what is involved in these dynamics and in moving along the road to their awareness.

Clearly there is no social component in the language investigation of the baby at the beginning of his life. His knowledge will be factual in terms of his use of what is available and what can be acted upon within himself. This approach to the potential will provide all the actual. To act on one component of the phonation system produces knowledge of what that component contributes on its own and, by involving it with others, knowledge of how its contribution is affected by those of others.

There are several thousand dialects on Earth, a fact that tells us that many, many uses of the same components are possible and have been selected from by human groups for the specific purpose of creating languages.

A baby who is not yet involved in social intercourse with the speakers of the language of his environment has no obligation to limit himself to the set of utterances selected for the group (for it is a limitation). He reaches a level of competence in using his vocal system that is most likely equal to the level of any speaker around, though he may not utter a single sound of the speaker's language when he "speaks" *his* own unique, un-understandable and most likely unrecorded language.

Talking is this set of activities, leading to the level of performance so many parents have noticed in their children at around their first birthday.

The sounds produced by the use of the vocal cords are the vowels whose distortions result from various frictions and from reflections on the walls of the mouth and on the funnel formed by the lips, all before the vowels reach the air beyond the mouth. Many vowels sound so like each other that they are easily confused. It is possible to conceive that the throat essentially only needs to generate about five vowels and that all the existing variations result from subsequent interferences from the other components used in uttering sounds.

The other sounds produced in the mouth all need air which has to pass through the opening of the larynx. If this opening is held so that no vowels are produced, the sounds that are generated result from the impact both of the air on some parts of the mouth and of those parts upon the air.

In the first months of life, when teeth are not yet available, a number of sounds that are affected only by the tongue, cheeks, palate and lips are still possible to make and are uttered by babies. Within the range of choices some are retained later but the knowledge of the remaining sounds becomes useless because they are not practiced. Since the acquaintance that each of us had with these "foreign" sounds was merely somatic, to try to produce these "foreign" sounds later may meet with failure—unless one can be assisted to regain the state that regenerates the "lost" knowledge.

5 Talking

For weeks or months a baby engaged in his utterances will be put in a position to become knowledgeable about all the variables that are part of these utterances. Their duration, their pitch and their intensity are three of the variables that babies can study, both in terms of the energy required, and through the analyzed impacts upon the ear. The two systems of criteria, independent of each other in the beginning, become mutually supportive and interchangeable.

Deaf people will stop at the development of the first system of energy variation and gain intelligence of what can be related to it when they are later taught the properties of sound through their eyes and skin. This intelligence, translated into orders to the still existing somatic functionings, produces sounds that the non-deaf can accept and feed back their acceptance so that the deaf continue using them.

For the non-deaf baby the two systems of conscious experiences, concerning utterances and impacts on the ear, are put into correspondence so that the ear and the mouth are functionally connected. The time needed to create this systematic correspondence is found in the crib when explicit experimentation takes place.

Babies have no difficulty in emitting a sound and noting its impact upon their ear. There is no danger that the baby will confuse this sound with the sounds of the environment since the utterance can take place at any time of the day or night—at those times when the baby knows himself to be left alone and can be sure that *he* and no one else has uttered *this* sound. He at once gives himself a test by doing it again, and, if need be, again and again.

Concentrating on both ends, the production of the sound and its reception, he knows what he does to make the utterance and almost at once he also perceives the particular alterations in his ear and the part of the brain connected with it. He can therefore keep the two awarenesses connected, or else voluntarily emit a sound and switch his attention to knowing it as an entity reaching his ear. When satisfied that his ear is as good an informant of what his throat does as his own direct contact with the throat (through consciousness), he can relax one of the watchers and leave one system to keep vigil over the functions of the phonation system. From then on the ear holds the feedback mechanism to inform consciousness of what the throat is doing when uttering sounds.

Every baby soon knows how to increase or reduce both the volume and the duration of any sound it can produce. These acts are distinct from the capability of stressing or ignoring a sound at will. Ignored earlier in a baby's life, sound now becomes a reality *per se* that consciousness can relate to. When the ear registers one of these sounds, the self acknowledges it for what it is. Repetition and the speed of successive utterances can also be related to and worked on. A somatic count of repeated sounds can take place because the maintenance of tracks in the memory is already possible, and indeed the coexistence of these tracks is a form of counting. The time between utterances is also somatically controllable so that every baby can slow down or speed up these voluntary utterances. The succession of noises has accompanied crying from the beginning of one's awareness of the world and all their variations were somatically noticeable.

Since each of us (people who can read and write included) recognizes the various sounds of our language as sounds regardless of all the other associations they may have for us, there must be objectively distinct properties of these sounds that strike us. (If need be, these properties can be shown on cathode ray tubes to prove their objective existence.) Sounds must therefore correspond to distinctive objective configurations of the phonation system, the result in turn of distinctive constellations of orders given to the constituent parts of the system. Each baby works on the generation of these constellations and ensures himself that they are available on call in the various states in which they can be produced: uttered slowly, uttered quickly; repeated; mingled with other mastered sounds, and so on.

Now, the provision of this spectrum of known sounds is a by-product of the work done both at the level of phonation or utterance, and at the level of the ear. But it now is a tool for the baby. The more elements there are in the spectrum the more can be done with it in terms of sounds *per se*.

For instance, an awareness of the possibility of uttering two different sounds one after the other carries with it the possibility of gaining the awareness that there are two orders for the succession of these sounds, and when sounded the perceptible differences in the two orders cannot escape notice. Thus, either deliberately or by chance, a baby can discover that the set of sounds he can utter allows of some combinations and permutations. Awareness of any change that makes combinations different can lead to the awareness that the change is equivalent to a substitution. Putting these observations together, we cannot say anything other than that babies can become aware of an *algebra* on the set of their utterances.

This awareness provides a power that finds its way into other fields of manifestation. Already when learning to order the various movements of his eyes, or when learning to order the command to his head to turn by definite amounts to catch a sound or a sight, there have been opportunities for a baby to know that these movements are ruled by an algebra in which, for example, movements can be composed to produce other movements, each movement can be canceled by an opposite movement, and each turning can be the outcome of a variety of choices of pairs of turnings.

Readers may feel awkward at the thought that we endow children so young with the capacity to become aware of algebras in their activities. We have no choice, except perhaps to refuse to name as algebra what babies actually do, though they are the same activities that mathematicians legitimately refer to as algebras when they are considering abstract sets structured by similar operations.

Babies learning to talk do have ample opportunity to relate consciously to the voluntary utterances they make. So how could they escape noticing that they add, subtract, substitute, reverse,

5 Talking

combine, repeat and re-order sounds? How can they escape systematizing their conscious work when the material is all in their hands and intimately known? Is it harder to notice these varieties than to notice what can be done with the ocular muscles or those in the neck?

In generating the thousands of known languages, humanity ultimately resorted to using a small number of sounds for each language—in other words, resorted to using an algebra to produce the many times more numerous words of each language. How could this occur at the beginning of the formation of a language if it was not an endowment of the linguistic mind, that is if it could not be noticed?*

To achieve all these awarenesses we do not need all the sounds of a language; a few can serve equally well. But the fact that no baby is committed to any language leaves him free to play with his powers and increase his arsenal of sounds as well as his arsenal of non-verbal (essentially non-substantive) components.

He can classify the sounds that make their appearance when the first teeth grow to the point where they grind against each other

---

* All languages use a small number of basic sounds, but each uses the combinations of these sounds. Languages recognize permutations of sounds as being temporally different, hence they accept them as being available for labeling differently perceived situations. They use a mental factory to produce any number of labels. Some languages use glottal stops, others use tonal distinctions, some use both, others distinguish sounds by making them longer or shorter, by repeating them distinctly, and so on—all awarenesses that are part of talking. Hence the real problems when studying the shift from talking to speaking are those related to how a very young child can discover that labeling exists and determine the laws of association for the many meanings that are attributed to particular words in dictionaries. In fact a baby has to reach the function of words at the same time that he suspects that a noise can be a substitute for pointing, or for the awareness of some feeling, or some more complex meaning like mother's disapproval of his behavior, etc.

and smooth off the saw-like edges that opened up slots in the gums. The dental sounds are played with now, as he played with the labial ones two or three months earlier, and the lingual and the palatal sounds in their time.

The ear now holds the clues that make the mouth capable of interpreting the sounds that it hears in terms of utterance. Since a baby can evoke all he knows, he can play at the virtual level the game of giving himself a symbolic sound, evoked in the ear or the brain, and then discover whether the organs of phonation take the position and shape necessary to produce the sound if they were actualized by an additional amount of energy.

The key to the entry into a language is in this apprenticeship: the study of the parts of the mouth which correspond to the sounds that are heard. Since one can hear sounds that cannot be uttered (such as thunder, or the noise of a car), babies are aware that what strikes them from the environment can be subdivided into distinctive classes according to whether the sound can be reproduced actually by them or only evoked virtually.

Languages are sounds related in time to form words and collections of words. Each language presents in the stress given to each word, in the melody of each sentence and in intonations, elements that can be reached *per se* without any reference to the labeling component. These extra-verbal elements—having an objective existence—will be reachable as soon as the baby's consciousness is touched by each of them.

But long before speaking his environment's language, each baby who hears has had the opportunity to note that users of the language utter sounds that are modulated by voices in a manner he has made himself capable of analyzing. He can dedicate himself to knowing as much as he wishes of this material and to learning to reproduce it virtually or actually. While doing this, he discovers that he uses *his* voice and not a copy of those he has heard, although he can evoke them and he can recognize them in actuality or in evocation.

This discovery is one that frees each baby from wanting to do exactly and literally what others do. Even if it was possible it is not required. Some actors, singular individuals, masters of impersonation, select elements of the voice of some celebrity and produce them sufficiently closely to create an illusion of the other's presence. These actors prove that had all babies chosen to impersonate the people around them, each of us would be speaking to those we address using our voice as they use theirs, and we would end up finally with a group of people having only one voice.

We must therefore grant to each baby that he knows very early that there are verbal and non-verbal elements in all languages and that it is easier to assimilate the latter first.

Each baby can not only obtain access to all the non-verbal elements of a language but he can also show his endowment as a linguist by managing to get as much meaning from what he hears as can be carried by accent, stress, intonation and melody, even if he gets no meaning at all from the lexicographic component.

To learn to talk covers all this for him.

To sum up this chapter, we can say that our approach to the activity of babies learning to talk has revealed that it cannot be achieved unless a very vigilant self is at work very diligently and intelligently on subtle material that must be known (by the self) as energy transformations in order to gain existence.

Since most of us end up ready to learn to speak around a year after birth, it must be during those months that we come to non-verbal conclusions about the best way to approach the language of our environment. The transfer of criteria for phonation from the throat and mouth to the ears is crucial, for we shall be affected through our ears as soon as we lend sense to what people around are saying and have to interpret what we hear in terms of utterance.

This delicate and most effective approach to the subtle material of language is best done at this age simply because consciousness is closest to the soma at the beginning of life. Depending on the extent of our individual dedication, we shall each of us give ourselves for the rest of our lives a greater or a lesser acquaintance with the functionings of the systems involved.

The great singers, the early prodigies of the voice as an instrument mastered in all its variety of performance, can arise anywhere from any milieu because their origin lies only in having cultivated more than others, at the stage when intimate acquaintance is possible, those vocal gifts that belong to everybody. In particular, they have mastered access to the mechanisms that integrate breathing and phonation, to those that prolong the emission of sounds, to those that affect the distribution of energy along the phrases and modulate them, to those that voluntarily blend the evocation of emotions with the other vocal elements all taken care of at the same time. All these attentions, easiest to acquire at an early stage in life, provide the basis for the rapid growth of their experience and serve to distinguish them from those who are attracted by other fields of experience and only learn enough of all these awarenesses to make them competent to learn to speak.

It is at this stage that one knows whether one has perfect pitch, for it is now that perfect pitch gains meaning, somatically and in awareness, and can be maintained. Perfect pitch means the capacity to hold intact, in the part of one's consciousness that is in contact with one's ears, the number of vibrations of the hairs in the inner ear affected by the vibrations of the air. To put a particular stress on the maintenance of this property, which is recognizable by the self since it is known to the self in terms of energy intake, is one of the possible dialogues with the soma that is available to the self when it is engaged in the analysis of what affects the ear. Not all of us seem to entertain such dialogue, but all could. Hence we are only more or less expert at knowing the pitch of a note heard and so manage to be no more than acceptable singers.

By a study in terms of temporal hierarchies it is possible to find out who has done a thoroughly good job at the level of what we have called talking, and given himself a chance to enter the universe of sound more secure and better equipped than other people.

Much more could have been said here about talking, but we leave some of it to the next chapter where it will gain more relief and will help to further our understanding of what we all did as children to gain our mastery of speech.

6 Speaking

Our separation of talking from speaking has allowed us to look at the apprenticeship of our native tongue as one that:

1 can be entirely carried out by each of us independently of others—except for their role as sources of noises having a number of accessible properties;

2 is followed by another apprenticeship that gives other people a considerable role.

Just as one does not say "I know swim" but "I know how to swim," so one does not usually say "I talk Spanish" but "I speak Spanish," indicating a difference in meaning that makes us select the word *speak* to stress that we are not acting independently. To speak is to learn to utter specific sounds that belong to others—in the sense that we do not invent the sounds but take them from the environment.

Most children who learn to talk end up learning to speak one of the codified languages used in their environment, however difficult that particular language seems to adults who learn it as a second, or foreign, language. Perhaps there is something in the phase of learning to talk that makes it easy to learn to speak later on.

We must not forget that all languages have a history even if their origins are lost in the past. However difficult it is to imagine people starting a language, it is easy to acknowledge that they have done so, more or less deliberately, with each generation adding something to the transmissions from previous generations. The evidence is around us every day.

To enter the spirit of the inventors of languages means to return to the awareness of talkers and to let them give permanence to some of their happy utterances which others could grasp and reproduce easily. If we notice that all spoken languages have objective features that characterize them and are reachable by anyone who manages to transform these aural characteristics into utterances, we see that to have learned to talk will also have made it possible to analyze the *noises* that are heard and attempt to produce them.

All those who learn to speak must use their own voices to produce those elements in the packets of energy received by the eardrums that we call words. It is obvious to every baby acquainted with sounds that words are carried by voices, and can only be reached by ignoring the attributes of voices that do not belong to the words. Hence no baby will imitate the voices he hears, although he could, but will on the contrary abstract words from their carriers and place them on his voice as their new vehicle. This is no metaphor. As we have seen in our studies

6 Speaking

in previous chapters, analysis and synthesis are part of every baby's functionings, and these two capabilities give a baby everything he needs to take words from others and make them his own.

Still, a baby cannot escape, any more than an adult, the fact that words have no meaning on their own; that they are either totally arbitrary or, in a few instances, formed of combinations of sounds that may have some somatic origin. It has been said, for example, that the Sanskrit word *Karma*, supposedly summing up one's destiny, starts with a guttural, at the source of phonation, is followed by the conveyor *r*, produced by the tongue, and ends up with the labial *m*, which puts the sound in the open as an explosion. But who can say that *inchoate* tells us anything of its meaning?

An illusion which many linguists indulge in can be found in the study of etymology. It says that words have meanings because some words of one language can be shown to be selected from words of another that convey meaning to those who know it. In fact "telephone" may be understood, if one knows Greek, to say "voice from far," but is this really the meaning of the noun *telephone* or of the actions summed up by the verb?

It is both correct in itself and safer for the consequences to assume that words have no meaning on their own. This can be ascertained at once by listening to a language one does not know. Hence every learner of a language has to learn that language must *first* have meanings to refer to and be able to understand how they have been labeled as they are in his environment.

Since babies have had access, since they were conceived, to very many meanings in the form of their perceptions of the surrounding world or of the dynamics in the bag, the problems they will have in establishing the meanings given to sounds are: first, awakening to the fact that people in the environment use sounds in non-arbitrary ways; second, recognizing that there are correspondences between what is uttered and what one perceives; third, recognizing that when the transformations are used (such as plurals), they are used deliberately and in order to achieve certain ends; fourth, recognizing that the more accurate and complex one's awareness of the world is, the more shaded are the meanings one finds there and the more numerous the need for new words to label them.

The bridge between talking and speaking can well be a chance occurrence, as seems to happen sometimes to all of us. While practicing his *nth* sound and amalgamation of sounds, a baby may be uttering a sequence of *dadada* or *mamama* or *papapa*... when an adult hears him and exclaims, "Listen, he is calling his father or his mother." And the adult may even believe it. Then all the family surrounds the baby and asks for encores, uttering the sounds the baby is practicing and is therefore acutely aware of.

Thus brought to the baby's awareness is the fact that his ears can recognize what is uttered not only by his mouth but by the mouths of others. He can now use the comb of the spectrum of sounds he has constructed to analyze what he hears and sees on the mouths of others. He can also now attempt to guide his utterances to evoke the sounds he has heard. His original utterances may be merely truncated replicas of those sounds. Yet although baby-talk is an incompetent rendition of what is heard, it is as faithful a production as the expertise of the talker allows. That so many babies produce the same "distorted" form of words from the environment cannot be due to chance; just as no one can produce dentals without teeth, no one is able to utter what he does not know how to utter. So babies doing, as usual, what they know, utter only what they find in the sounds they hear—those elements that they can recognize through their ear and their throats.

But because the spectrum of sounds expands and listening is acute, babies correct themselves and constantly improve their performance. This improvement is deliberate, the outcome of a reflective self. Some words of the language of the environment are produced correctly at once. This is the case with those words that are repeated syllables, like *papa, mama*. Some other words suggest an entry into their production and babies try using their breath to produce what their ear catches and their mouth can produce. Still others are not even attempted: they are not yet recognizable to the analytic system formed at that time.

While this goes on at the level of utterances, another dialogue is set on course. Babies who have perceived so much of the intricate organization of the surrounding world can also perceive that there are concomitant utterances and gestures made by everyone around. For example, "give it to me," "no," "take this," are so often associated with visible indices that can strike the attentive baby, that he turns things around and tests his comprehension by offering his version of the sounds he believes he should utter and waits for the feedback.

Once he starts on this road, he can easily acquire what he guessed correctly and tested thoroughly to his own satisfaction, and can "reflect" on how he did it and for what results. Increased awareness of the field both precedes and follows each attempt—the one that precedes makes the attempt possible, the one that follows makes one surer, bolder, and, particularly, more sensitive on many more fronts.

Babies learning to speak know that they don't yet know all the answers, and do not pretend that they do. As usual their attitude of suspended judgment, their keen awareness coupled with selective concentration on elements related to their knowledge, and their focus on perception, makes things happen. Rather than trial-and-error or chance learning, the child's method is that of directed learning which feeds back every piece of progress and makes the child know that he has achieved a definite, certain end, even when the end is not the aim of the project. Such is the flexibility of the engagement of consciousness in the act of learning that it can be moved without difficulty to another matter that seems interesting.*

---

* Who has not taken for intellectual superficiality or immaturity the ease with which young children leave an occupation, including the experience of deep grief, to be utterly taken by what has just met their perception? This power of babies, and sometimes of older children, to identify with a task immediately, is a tool of such importance in learning that we should all acquaint ourselves with it.

6 Speaking

Children, although they end up speaking more or less equally well, start at different ages and follow different routes; they dwell longer in some areas than in others because they find something fascinating in them. Numerals, for instance, may strike one child as having some property resembling the physical learning of climbing steps, and he may master counting, say, at the age of two before he gives signs that he has mastered a sentence, thereby making the task of counting seem to be so easy for some younger children.

(The particular task of counting involves a very specific set of demands to be mastered: twelve noises, say, must be retained; they must be put in order; they must then be synchronized with a somatic complex that includes lifting a leg from one step and putting it on the next and then, with the help of the arm on the banister, lifting the whole body to that level. However complicated a behavior, it is a limited one and is open to a two year old who engages himself with its components.)

No real learning takes place without the gift of oneself to that which has to be integrated. To be wholly dedicated to an interest is a *sine qua non* condition for the self to be fair to itself and to the task at hand. Young children know this intensity and use it systematically, thus producing the huge increase in knowing and knowledge of the early years. Nowhere is it more needed than in learning to speak because speech is in time, because speakers rarely utter one word at a time, because words have no meaning on their own, because consciousness is hidden behind statements and a constant shift of the listener's mind may be required to grasp the meaning of a statement.

The intellectual demand of a sequence of words in time is multiple. We have to hear each word when it strikes the ear, we have to retain it while we shift to the next word, we have to do this a number of times until the statement is finished, and then hold this statement in the mind to draw out of it its meaning.

Once meaning is squeezed out of a statement, the words do not need to be remembered, and the recovery of the energy mobilized for that task begins. Memory of words heard fades quickly and cannot be relied upon.

If this is what we all have to do to take in speech, it must also be done by babies, unless someone proves that learning to speak requires a succession of approaches discarded one after the other in favor of the next better one.

The way babies find a solution to the challenge of speaking is characteristic. They begin with one-word statements. "No" is an especially convenient such statement, for it conveys meanings while simultaneously protecting the baby-utterer from the aggression of the loving environment and asserting him as a will.*

---

* Babies use "no" systematically, not only to reject environmental pressure and interference, but also to discover what is behind the arbitrary sounds floating around. Because speech is in time and because it is only a vehicle for meaning for the user, the learner of speech who has missed something that he feels the need for so as to make more sense of the world, must resort to some strategy and some tactic to recreate the lost opportunity. "No" is one of his instruments to have the whole thing dished out again. Normally he will not use it if all is well, if he is content with an intuition and can Progress in his work. But how would he otherwise capture that which has vanished into the past? He discovered early enough in his talking that repetition is available to him; now he gets it from others by triggering it with a mere "no." (Still, this discovery requires

But quite a number of such statements are possible, even if they are not part of the environmental speech habits. If "go," "come," "take" and "eat" are conventional, "give" is not, "hand" is not, "spoon," "alone," . . . are not. Babies choose to utter what they can manage, and by trying out what is convenient to them, they gain an entry into the correspondence of sound to meaning and also to the converse. The environment, delighted by any such feat, responds enthusiastically to sounds that, even though truncated, are related to what appearances suggest is an appropriate context for those sounds.

The tolerance of the environment is very helpful to the baby, for once the correspondence between sound and meaning is sufficiently established so that he can release his attention from this task, he can go on with his task of improving utterances.

A baby must do the whole of this work on his own. The environment is so far removed from what he does that all its guesses about his utterances may be wrong, and deliberate help may mean only hindrance. Hence the attitude that anything offered by a baby is miraculous and thus has to be accepted with grace, is the best support that parents can give their children in this field.

---

special conditions to become a weapon against the environment. It has this potential, but it does not necessarily develop into it.)
In the course of a "no"-triggered exchange, baby and adult are engaged in a dialogue that has utterly different meanings for both. While the adult concentrates on the message, the baby concentrates on the vehicle that conveys that message. His is a more complex task, and according to circumstances he may neglect the message in order to be more with the vehicle. The environment, so ignorant of the ways of knowing available to a child, so unconcerned with the enormous task he is engaged in, has little interest in helping and often hinders by interpreting the actions of the learner as sheer ill-will. Later, "what?" will play a role similar to "no" and can also become a tool for a nagging child to infuriate his parents.

In families with more than one child, parents often turn to their children to decode what the youngest child utters when he is a newcomer to speech. This decoding is possible between children because of the older child's remaining awareness into the process of learning, an awareness that gradually gets buried with age.

In all households love is a better inducement to children to learn to speak than their own need for communication. In fact communication has little to do with learning to speak. Young children's needs have been taken care of for millennia without a word being exchanged between offspring and parent.

Newcomers do not know how or why the environment developed its language, but they find the organization of sounds called language as much a part of the environment as trees or fields. They find in themselves the know-hows that allow them to acquire a system of sounds that serve in certain circumstances as substitutes for meanings. If there is a single need met by language, it is the tendency to replace actions that are expensive in energy by others that are far less expensive. It costs less to tell someone how to reach a place than to take him there. It takes less energy to enquire verbally about what may be required to reach a particular end than to embark upon the actions leading to it.

Language is a luxury, not a necessity, but one the sons of men seem to be able to afford and which transforms them into wealthy people—wealthy, that is, in terms of higher potential energy.

6 Speaking

Once man had become aware of the economy that a code of verbal signs represents, he embarked upon the road of developing languages as different from each other as that activity permits, with nothing but talking as a prerequisite for the task. Man can live without language, but he prefers to make use of what makes him capable of inventing one. The invention itself exemplifies the attributes of the minds that will allow it to be used.

At school we are taught grammar as a formal study of the rules of language and many students find it uninteresting or difficult. But no baby could learn his environment's language if he did not make himself sensitive to the many components of grammar—to all of them, in fact. Every baby is properly equipped for such a complicated job because he knows how to suspend judgment, he knows how important it is to give himself to a task, to pay attention, to focus on some point in order to master it, to interpret feedback, etc. He is as sure of the fluctuating nature of the outside world as of his own experience, and he uses his intellectual powers so efficiently that as soon as he knows a little he manages to know a lot.

Because of all this, sometime in less than a year, a one-year-old child learns to speak a language that has taken centuries to evolve to that point. The child's awareness, of course, is of learning the language, not of the history or evolution of that language, but it is still an awareness of all that is being used to make that language what it is.

We must therefore look at the learning in terms of what is required by the material and how it is supplied by the child himself, keeping both in mind. Sometimes what the child supplies will be a guess, sometimes a stressing or an ignoring of attributes, sometimes the generation of a special sensitivity. As we have seen, all this is done consciously, deliberately, and learned for good when the feedback assures that it is safe to automate the operation by using the many subtle high-speed machines available in the bag.

Spontaneously suspending judgment and the awareness that meanings must be deliberately attached to sounds, make children think in terms of the vastest categories, and they move towards closing in on particular meanings by processes that force clusters of words to work in coordinated ways. The construction of language by children for the purpose of expressing what is consciously held in the mind makes it possible to learn such a complex system. The construction is systematic, using all that is available: intelligence, mental instruments, sensitivities, different ways of knowing, postponements, etc.

Because it is a construction it can be analyzed and it can reveal how children learn to speak any language in the environment. Once more, awareness is the illumination that provides minutely detailed answers.

Awareness of function linked to sensitivities leads to awareness of vocabulary and the classification of words by their various functions, linked to memory. To learn to speak as well as all

6 Speaking

children manage can only be possible if each of them does the right things.

Although no one can invent the vocabulary selected by the environment, there is a great deal of creative activity in learning to speak and a great variety in the solutions to the problem of acquiring an existing language. If freedom were not part and parcel of this apprenticeship, the uniqueness of human beings could not be accommodated. Circumstances differ every day for each of us; what people say is unpredictable; so are the demands of situations. Hence there is no one-track program to be followed by all children, not even the babies in any one family. Conversely, the simple fact that all children learn to speak eliminates the existence of a single program in language learning. Instead, as always, there are temporal hierarchies: the construction of islands of connected awarenesses corresponding to certain criteria and vocabularies, which are then related to chunks of experience in the world and to sections of the world; the construction of continents out of these separate islands; the construction of verbal universes with the presence of a unique self in them using what was given in a unique fashion. Though speech is assimilated from the environment, it becomes part of one's substance, is in one's bag intimately connected with all the talking apparatus, and it finds new uses for somatic elements to perform—such as retaining words, and keeping alive their links to images, feelings, thoughts, etc.

Since adults verbalize spontaneously all the time they provide each child, who is watchful of what happens in the environment, with a large number of opportunities to acknowledge that the sounds he hears uttered by adults are sometimes mysterious and unrelated to anything he can perceive, and at some other times concomitant with what he can notice. Nouns are of this last kind, and he may associate the sound "doggy" with the animal he is familiar with, "glass" with the object used by everybody at meals. But he can also notice that "eat" always recurs when someone is feeding him, and although he cannot use the word because he does not feed people, the possibility is open to him to make sure of its meaning. He simply tests that the word is uttered again if he refuses to open his mouth, and again and again, and used not only by his mother but by anyone confronted with his refusal to open his mouth.

As he continues to work on relating meaning to words that are meaningless *per se*, and sorts out the words attached to objects and those attached to actions, he can relate to speech in a variety of ways. Besides words as such, he has entry to the staccato of phrasing and the temporal form of the melody of the language, to the stressing of words and the use of intonation in sentences.

Since he can mobilize himself on one or more of these characteristics, he will find that to speak (that is, to produce the complex of sounds produced by the people of his environment) he needs to synthesize the components that he can reach separately. How could he therefore *not* know that the imperative form of a verb requires that he be directed in a total way to the awareness associated with a command about opening his mouth (eat!), moving his whole body (come!), bending his head when being shampooed (bend!), turning his head to let mother see whether the ears are clean (turn!), etc. The concomitants of the voice force awareness both of a verbal form (here the imperative) and of the particular sound as it relates to the particular action he is involved in. The perception of these components leads to the development of a sensitivity to the function of words, wider than the process of paying a particular *ogden*,* that will make a particular word available for a long time to come.

The perception of an object as belonging to a class—that, say, a collie is a dog just as a dachshund is—is possible because of the fact that we know *only* classes of impressions that are perceived to belong to each other, and thus we produce the concept of an object with only enough precision to accommodate all the related impressions. The same "looseness" that goes with the percepts-objects connection is associated spontaneously with words and remains a property of vocabulary. It is a necessary association. Words can be submitted to some vocal transformations without affecting what has been acknowledged to be their meaning (for example, when spoken by louder or softer voices), while some other transformations will affect the meaning (for example, when used to warn, to threaten, to promise . . .). All this educates every baby to watch for all the components that maintain or affect meaning, adding further to the complexity of the task, but also adding power to the tool that is forged. The power of make-believe, present in some of the behavior of even nine-month-old babies, can be integrated with speech in dialogues a baby can carry on with any object made into a toy (or with a doll given to the child). It is the basis of symbolism.

---

* The name I gave to a unit of learning involved in retaining something invented by others.

To comprehend nouns the learning child must associate classes to them simply because he knows that the world is not ruled by him and that he cannot call a thing by any word he chooses. His mistake of addressing any male visitor as "dad" reveals his state of mind and shows the conflict between his learning of nouns and, in this case, some social factor that he has not yet perceived. Although all dogs are called "dog"—and using "dog" for a cat (easily taken to belong to the same class) is normal in this context—the use of "dad" for every person is forbidden, for the word refers to an invisible characteristic, a relationship that will be met again and again, thus generating a class, but this time a class of pairs of individuals. The baby using words must refrain from using "dad" for every man, but will accept later that each person can use "dad" when referring to different people (in a few exceptional situations, to the same person). The shock of the awareness that nouns are for classes of individual objects and also for classes of pairs keeps each baby alert, which in turn helps make the learning of the language possible.

Awareness of lability, of transformation, is necessary in order to penetrate the mysteries buried in languages by their inventors. Pronouns are substitutes for nouns; there are very few pronouns compared with the many nouns, and they are "passe-partout" words. "I" can be used by everyone but it means someone else when heard and means oneself when uttered. Pronouns are used continually by the environment and because they are small words that can be isolated from the rest, they usually get attention quite early. "I" is an exception, and offers difficulties of another kind. Awareness of oneself is normal and is present from the start. Further, the subject can become aware of his actions as well as of himself as an object (*me*). But for the subject to name himself as if he were an object, and with a label different from "me," provides a considerable challenge that is normally solved only when children have been speaking for some time.

When we confront these difficulties as actual obstacles to babies, their examination opens up new vistas for further investigation of languages and their apprenticeship.

It is extremely difficult to conceive of how to make a young child who cannot say "I" reach the awareness that makes the word an obvious one to use. Still, because children end up saying "I" like everybody else in the environment, a path must be available to them, and therefore to us in our investigation.

Parents call children by their given name, or some nickname, and this attribute soon becomes associated with the child's awareness of himself. He can even shift without difficulty from that name to the pronoun the language uses to address someone else ("you" in English). But he cannot use "you" to refer to himself, although others can. He hears himself being called "him," and notices he is not addressed on these occasions. To this he acquiesces easily. So for his own use he either resorts to his given name or to "me," which are interchangeable. Others can say "give Jim" or "give him," and he can correspondingly say "give me" or "give Jim." Only when he has worked out enough examples, sorting out the acceptability of his utterances to the environment by its feedback, is he able to make linguistic sense of the fact that others can sometimes be heard to say "I" and sometimes their own name, and that when "I" is used the speaker does not say his own name: all of which is accessible to his perception and his intelligence.

Once this is understood, the awareness of subject and object as distinct grammatical functions is secured forever. (They are interchangeable only in the idioms of some dialects. In English, for example: "You are a liar." "Who? Me?")

In some languages we find that "I" is buttressed by "me" (in French it is permissible to say "Moi, je . . ." as the subject), while in other languages personal pronouns are conceived as redundant and omitted, except for emphasis, because the form of the verb tells unequivocally who the subject is (as in Spanish).

In the case of possessive pronouns there are two elements of a sentence to be replaced by the pronoun; for example, "my glass" becomes "mine."

Beginning the process of learning demonstrative pronouns, children quite early say, "I want this and this and this," while pointing at some candies or cookies; they recognize that it is possible to convey meaning without the nouns. They keep these forms ("this," "that," etc.) in mind, thinking that the noun is unnecessary since pointing replaces naming. Awareness of the demonstrative pronoun is thus born and can be made part of one's use of the language.

Some pronouns have the same sound as the corresponding adjective; for example, the word *this* in "This egg is painted and this is not." The same meaning is conveyed by both clauses in

"This book goes here and this one there" and can be conveyed by the same sentence without the word "one."

Pronouns are accepted easily because substitution is one of the transformations long practiced by babies. At the same time they provide an economy of words and so agree with the general dynamics of consciousness, which always leads to more being done for less.

Adjectives are the labels for attributes recognizable by sense organs. Photons have been received by the retina for so long, that they are directly known by the brain. But words do not exist in sufficient numbers to describe each of them univocally. So photons are lumped together as they appear to be in the rainbow, *grosso modo*, and a few words are used to name collections of colors although, in fact, so many exist.

The eye can perceive shape and color at the same time just as it can perceive colors and hues. Stressing and ignoring attributes produce awarenesses of one, or the other, or both.

On the whole, each separation of awareness is matched with a distinction in vocabulary and these verbal units can only be used as a succession of words in time and not as a way of transmitting the simultaneity of experience. Speakers and hearers get used to the difference between (one-unit-after-another) speech and (total) awareness; conjunctions are the verbal tool for handling the difference and making hearers wait.

Simultaneous perception leads to the verbalization of the perceived attributes. Since attributes are known to be coexistent, adjectives are used to describe qualifying situations, there being as many possible adjectives as there are attributes. The vocabulary for these attributes is learned as the opportunities occur, not systematically in a prescribed order from a list.

A child may acquire the word "red", and then not encounter and retain a word for another color for some time. The absence of any other color label has nothing to do with a lack of perception of all the colors that photons bring to one's eyes. In the same way, "flat" and "round" may be learned at about the same time, while other comparable properties may be perceived but not labeled. A child possessing these words can label and relate a round red object or a red flat object, and he may even be able to label a red flat round object or a round flat red object.

Now, behind these dynamics, accessible to a child who gives evidence of perceiving attributes, there is something that is known in mathematics as the Venn diagrams. They describe exactly what is asked of children who have to master the use of adjectives in any language.

First we learn to pair adjectives with their opposites (when they exist). Cold and hot, tall and short, thick and thin, light and heavy, etc. These are mutually exclusive pairs, although there are boundary areas where one would not know which label to choose.

6 Speaking

No object can have at the same time any two of these attributes, and the classes of mutually exclusive attributes can be represented by areas of the plane which neither touch nor overlap (Figure 1).

But they can also have attributes belonging to different pairs, in which case there would be overlapping areas representing the classes of objects having two or more of these attributes (Figure 2).

Since all colored objects have at least one color, if we represent the class of colored objects by an area, it can be subdivided into subclasses—each for one color. The result can also be looked at backwards, in the sense that the areas allocated to each color can be brought together to produce the *union* of the areas, which would cover exactly what was allocated to the class of colored objects (Figure 3).

Fig. 1

Illustrates the extension of two classes A_1 and A_2 of objects whose attributes are mutually exclusive (e.g. round and square).

The notational form for this is,

$A_1 \cap A_2 \sim \phi$

$\cap$ says that the elements common to the two classes are considered

ϕ means empty

Fig. 2

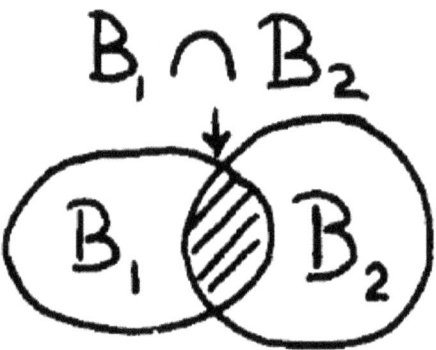

Illustrates the fact that there may be two classes B_1 and B_2 of objects whose attributes can be compatible (e.g. round and red).

$B_1 \cap B_2 \neq \phi$

$B_1 - B_1 \cap B_2$ and

$B_2 - B_1 \cap B_2$ are not empty and represent what is left of a class when a part is removed

Fig. 3

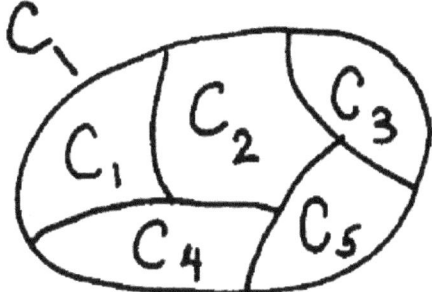

Illustrates a partition of a class C into mutually exclusive subclasses $C_1, C_2, \ldots C_n$ (e.g. colored objects can be subdivided into red, yellow . . .).

$C \sim C_1 \cup C_2 \cup C_3 \cup \ldots C_n$ is the notation for this *union* of the parts to produce the whole

Fig. 4

Illustrates the case of a subclass being separated within a class by the simultaneous consideration of a further attribute (e.g. among red objects D, the round ones form D_1, and D_2 is formed of all others).

In notation:

$$D \sim D_1 \cup D_2$$

$$D_1 \sim D \cap D_1$$

$$D_2 \sim D \cap D_2$$

No child, of course, formalizes his apprehension of adjectives in this mathematical way, but as soon as he proves that he can use adjectives like everybody else he has the necessary perceptive and conscious experience to serve as a foundation for this formulation. In fact, as soon as children speak a little, parents teach them to label opposites and even play games of words with them. As a result children pass on to their verbal awareness what they already have in their sensibility. Children will accept "a black and white horse" but not "a totally black horse that was totally white." The world of attributes having its perceptible criteria, these criteria are associated with the vocabulary of the attributes.

Children who have made the transfer from one system to the other can believe the words as much as their perception. So words exclude each other as much as do sensations, and loyalty to words replaces the loyalty to the truth of perceptible experience. In this sense, words become realities as consistent as sensations.

As already suggested *and* and *or* are the conjunctions of this part of experience and are associated in the mind with simultaneity and alternation.

As for adverbs, they too refer to perceptible components of experience, and they allow young children to stress them and isolate them in their consciousness. Adverbs are first recognized to exist in some particular cases and then, as they are for grammarians, qualifiers of verbs. As soon as the meaning of an action is associated with a verb and the variations of actions are recognized, adverbs are learned at the same time as the verb they qualify. The experience of walking more or less fast provides two vectors—one increasing speed, the other decreasing it. To these two perceptions, the words *quickly* and *slowly* will be associated respectively. *More* and *less* will also be experienced, not only as adverbs.

Prepositions are of particular significance. They indicate perceptions of relationships in space and time. There are many such relationships, and the existence of words for each of them adds opportunities for noting them. This is one example of the two-way traffic between perception and language. The first is needed to make sense of the second, and the need to make sense of it develops awarenesses that might otherwise escape notice.

Once the speakers of a language have noted that speech is an effective tool of expression—in that the systems of sounds and the non-verbal components represent to one's satisfaction what one has in mind—they will use it in one way when they refer to past experience and in another way to refer to the future. As with the other elements of speech, awarenesses must first exist before a need is generated to produce speech forms for their expression. Hence every baby who, like any adult, knows that something talked about is being evoked rather than perceived, will know what it is that makes him notice the words that refer to the past, and he will establish a sensitivity to tenses in the flow of words. The referentials, being repeatedly used, become second nature, and criteria at the level of speech replace criteria of awareness. A particular sound enclosed among others that form a sentence (uttered or heard), can trigger only the inner climate that is compatible with the meanings associated with some of the words. Thus we reject, "I'll see you yesterday," but accept, "I'll see you later," even though the sentences have the same valid form.

For a young child, as for the adult, it is the inner transformations of the self that make them "correct"—and that enables them to be passed by the internal censors that have changed criteria into automatic feedback mechanisms.

Of particular significance in the apprenticeship of the tenses and moods of verbs is the moment when the power of evocation comes together with an awareness that past, present and future coexist. The juxtaposition creates the form of the tenses. Placing the triad of past, present, and future on to each term of the triad generates the simple tenses, if the triad is placed on the present, and the compound tenses if it is placed on the past or the future, all of these comprising the indicative mood.

Children in their first three years or so show that they are busy in understanding consciously how the tenses are formed and very many English-speaking children deliberately interfere with the language. They regularize past tenses and say "breaked" for "broke" or "broken," "taked" for "taken," "teared" for "torn," etc., although they do not hear these words said. Such initiative must inevitably force students of early childhood to stop thinking that the act of learning one's native language is the result of simply saying what the people in the environment say.

In fact, without a clear concept of "relativity" young children would not learn the use of, say, possessive adjectives and pronouns. If a mother says to a baby, "This is *your* nose," why should *he* not say the same words when pointing at his nose? Instead, he changes the expression and says, "This is *my* nose." If he hears, "you are on my right," what he must finally say is, "I am on your left," a sentence that contains only the word *on* in common with the previous one.

Through their intellectual powers children invent more than the regular forms for the past tense of irregular verbs. They may be struck by other forms they hear and try to use them to express what they feel. All parents have scores of examples to illustrate this observation of the verbal initiative of young children. The following example is crystal clear: a boy, having at some point heard his mother say to him, "Come with me," and having heard himself say, "me talking," or, "and me," knows that *me* can be used by other people and by himself to refer to the speaker. On other occasions he may note that "both" is used to refer to two people or two things simultaneously Thus, he may take his mother's hand and say, "*both of me* go down to get the mail." Logically, "both of me" is as correct as "both of us," but only the latter has been adopted.

The real criterion for knowing a language is the capacity to transform statements that are heard into the proper, and perhaps very different, statements that must be uttered by a speaker to convey the same meaning.*

The conscious ingredients that make every child who hears learn to speak the language of his environment in his early childhood are:

1. a mastery of all that we have discussed under the label of *talking*;

2. an enhancement of sensitivities so that perceptions of all kinds assist in the task of stressing *the function of words* and allows the isolation of what one has to focus upon—this makes every baby into a practicing grammarian;

3. the construction of multiple classifications of words according to the role they play in statements so that one can place the same word among the nouns or the adjectives or the adverbs and use it accordingly;

---

* At a certain age, children who are still learning the basics of their native language want to give themselves the criterion by which to judge whether they can produce as good a flow of words as their older siblings or their parents. They then play the game of "echoing," with the same speed and intonations, everything that people around them say. From single words to pairs and triplets of words, a novice speaker may note that, just as phrasing is a melodic component of uttered statements, stringing together bits of sentences is an open device to produce statements that express more precisely what one sees, feels, wishes, etc. Echoing provides the vehicle, and thus echoing belongs to talking rather than speaking.

For weeks on end children test their ability to utter anything and everything they hear immediately after it is uttered by someone else. This very annoying echo creates tension in homes where it is not understood as being a reasonable way of making sure that certain components of speech (flow and intonations) are mastered. Even when the meaning is clearly not their concern, children echo.

But as abruptly as it was taken up, it is dropped, and echoing reappears only much later as a game, or in order to annoy someone deliberately.

4 recognizing that awareness of living, or of evocation, or of anticipation, generates the awareness of words that represent the present, the past and the future as tenses;

5 recognizing that oneself can be both subject and object;

6 recognizing that one can be engaged in a variety of activities distinguishable from each other and that they are therefore generally labeled differently;

7 recognizing that attributes can either be isolated and labeled separately or evoked together and coordinated;

8 recognizing that almost all activities can be affected by one's will and thus that verbs can be modified by adverbs;

9 knowing that without awareness of relativity, vocabulary cannot be transformed to replace the forms applied by the environment to oneself;

10 a suspended-judgment attitude that provides *classes* of impressions as support for nouns, and an *algebra of classes* (similar to the algebra of adjectives but structured in terms of subclasses) to deal with classes qualified by adjectives; for example: the class of cars is made up of the classes of convertibles, sedans, two-door, etc., or of the cars of various makes, etc.

Without this basis of classes, algebra, and relativity, *no one* can learn as complicated a system as a language, which has developed over centuries and applies to all sorts of life situations. Children do not know that they use such intellectual tools, but they know the tools are needed and will be reached by them; they can find them through the dynamics of awareness. Instead of employing the above labels for what he must use to crack the code of his language, each baby develops stressing and ignoring as a dynamics, suspended judgment as a means of keeping classes open, and a simultaneous awareness that is the basis for the conjunction of a number of composing elements; and he moves ahead from one-word statements to longer and longer statements, made first by stringing together juxtaposable statements, and then by constituting more sophisticated statements—those in which what is to come can affect what has been said already.

This last performance we must study more closely.

Very early in one's life it is discovered that concatenation of actions exist:

- *mother goes into the kitchen . . . to prepare a meal;*
- *a bottle is brought . . . to be placed in one's mouth . . . to provide the drink . . . and when empty to be taken away . . . and sometimes placed on a table until the next request for a drink;*
- *one goes to the bathroom . . . to take a bath . . . to be dried and dressed;*
- *one goes to bed . . . to sleep;*

and many more.

Hence babies' evocations can have the same temporal structure as the related actions, even if the evocations are thought out in a flash. It is this receptacle of experience, the awareness of such conjunctions, that prepares children for the capacity to make lengthy statements (once they have secured the "verbal molecules" that correspond to shorter awarenesses).*

Children learning English no doubt note that what they one day see as a separate word has been part of statements often heard and used earlier; for example, "look at this" or "look for it" or "look up," "look down." A whole collection of prepositions becomes available as soon as "look" is isolated as a word.

Rather than making these multi-word verbs by composition, children acknowledge them as one unit, and only after using them for months do they find that other units of speech, used in other contexts, are also present in them. A child always hearing, "Be careful!," from anxious parents, may say, "I am becarefulling," showing competence in verb formation but not yet the awareness that there are two words in what he hears. Such awarenesses can be forced by the insertion of other words. "Be *as* careful as you can," may be one such device. But on the whole, even if the awarenesses are forced, they do not concern the important task of making statements out of a number of classes.

To construct statements the analysis-synthesis process, used from the beginning of life, is put to work on the verbal level, and

---

* In this non-verbal awareness is also to be found the basis for a firm grasp of key words such as "that," "which," "who," "whose," "what," etc., which are inherently ambiguous since they can have more than two functions; for example, "which" can be either an adjective or a pronoun, relative or interrogative.

here too it proves to be the decisive problem solver. The baby remains in contact with the whole challenge, holds it in his mind and scans it, stressing what he chooses and ignoring what he chooses. The result is a structuring by the will of the statements he hears in terms of some perceptible property that "colors" parts of the statement and produces a "relief" of it. Later on, because of these abilities, a baby will have the criteria that tell him that this is what "they" say, and that encourage him to retain the statement as well as his own attempts to produce statements evocative of an imagery which is compatible with the imagery he has already associated with the words.

A few associated comments:

Babies learn to speak because they do all the right things in agreement with the rest of their investigations of the surrounding world. They perceive truth and know that words are labels not to be confused with the things associated with them.

But the same sense of truth tells them that in certain situations some words are indicators of a concomitant state or presence, and they learn to use these words as "symbols" for that kind of reality and no longer just as "signs" of it. For some time there is hesitancy in accepting signs as symbols, but repeated experience tells the child that the associations to these signs are always present when the words are uttered, and the associations, not the sign, are what matter. Hence some words become symbols and carry with them occult meanings that take years to be fathomed. The words of religion, or of the areas that are taboo for one's community, are not just words like any others in the physical environment.

Speech that was an instrument for expression and was useable in a number of communications, can now serve esoteric ends. It becomes a code for the initiated. As soon as a sect or special group is formed, it adapts the language to its ends.

This is possible because the inventors of language made it vague enough to accommodate all expressible needs. They know that language as a code has properties accessible to all and yet that everyone sees the world from his own viewpoint, egocentric by definition. Such a perspective, in fact, accommodates every newcomer, who picks up his language usually before discarding his diapers.

Expressible experience can now be translated at once into an addition of new vocabulary and sometimes into new structures. No one says that the latter is not permissible. In fact all users of language consider the language their own. Children prove their ownership by creating secret codes among themselves; for example, by inserting the sound "egg" before each vowel of a word—a simple enough rule that alters radically the feel of the language and creates a sense of confusion in non-players, as if the secret language were a foreign language. Still, children manage to master such a code much faster than most adults, indicating that they are still very close to the sources of language learning.

We must also note that it is relatively easy for children in their early childhood to learn to speak a number of languages to a certain level of efficiency. The level will relate to the environment's use of the language, not to the children's personal competences. If the environment requires an equally refined use of all the languages that are spoken, multi-lingualism can result, and children do not know which is their native language since all the languages have been mastered equally well. It is possible to conceive of an environment where adults deliberately replace the value of supremacy for one language with the value that their children should know as many languages as possible to the same level of competence.

This is not expecting too much because the greatest job in learning to speak is done for one language and can be simply transferred to other languages. Vocabulary acquisition is the least of the demands in the learning of a new language. Hence if we learn languages at a time when we are intimately engaged in the study of one, we find access to all the others just as easily. If we start to meet language early there is no loss of the necessary powers when we go from one language to the next, and to the next. This power is what takes us from one language to another, not memory of words and rules, which can only represent obstacles in the new language. Nor do these powers disappear. We can maintain the capacity for learning more languages to any age.

To sum up the substance of this chapter, we can say that we have looked at how, in the task of learning to speak, consciousness alone can complete so complex a job as sorting out the manifold demands that are encountered and can develop the proper, adequate tools in terms of sensitivity, functioning, observation, daring, testing, and acceptance of adequacy.

The example of learning to speak is a valuable illustration of the powers of children; it also shows us that the conscious self alone can do this enormous job while other tasks are being worked on at the same time. The conscious self is the same one that did the various jobs in the soma, and the one that will do the many jobs to come. After learning to speak, that self not only finds itself owning a language that can be used but, more importantly, finds itself with the techniques of learning which were deliberately developed to meet and integrate that specific unknown.

7 Learning Other Things

We gave a great deal of attention to the acquisition of language because its study permitted us to develop new instruments of research and because it has remained a challenge for scientists for so long. The previous chapter reveals children as very skilled learners; their awareness turns to what can solve their problems and does not allow itself to be distracted. There are many examples of such learning in early childhood; adults are mostly unaware of their existence and their meaning for growth.

A principle that can serve us well, when we are looking at young children investigating their world, is *the need to know*. Much of what looks like idle play is the methodical examination of an unformulated question. The question becomes clearer to the observer if he stops sticking to a hypothesis of idle play and tries to ask: "What does the child need to know that he can get from this?"

In many kitchens where pots and pans are within reach of babies it is possible to see one of them concentrate on playing with this equipment for days if mother allows him and no other brother or sister spoils the game. What is there to find out in a set of pots and pans?

If they have lids, can one learn to know, simply by looking, which lid belongs to which pan? And if only one belongs to a particular pan are there traits of the others that can be isolated and make it possible to classify the lids in a series?

Can one pan be put inside another? When it is possible to do so, can one reverse the order? Can one involve all the pans in one series?

If the lids are involved, can we arrive at an arrangement that includes all the pans and the largest number of lids?

Is there only one solution?

Can one learn this in a manner that extends the power of one's mind, that is, allows one to see that, whatever answers were found, there were also awarenesses that were valid not only for these pans?

At any stage in this study the baby could be diverted and make concomitant discoveries. The noise (that terrible noise for the environment) can become the object of the baby's attention. Do lids vibrate when struck? What stops the vibration? How long is it perceptible if left to continue? Is the noise made by a lid that is too small to cover a particular pan different from the noise made by a larger lid when the two fall on, or touch, a given pan? How does one release a lid or a pan to produce the loudest sound in the various combinations of pans and lids? Is this sound affected by the distance the lid travels? Does the height from which a lid is dropped affect the noise it makes? Does the energy with which it is handled affect the level of noise? Can one strike a number of pans and produce recognizable sounds? Is the kitchen filled only with noise or can a kind of harmony be produced?

What about the weight of the pots and pans? Can one's hand lift any of them? Where does one place one's fingers? Is the thumb treated in a special way? Is one hand sufficient? If not, where must the second hand be placed to make lifting the smoothest, the fastest, the least tiring?

Of course, not all children go through the same experiences or ask the same non-verbal questions, but all get involved in games with household appliances that permit them to ask similar questions and to work towards complete answers.

Every child, being a learning system, goes straight to every situation in order to explore what can be known about it. To know finished products it is necessary to analyze them by breaking them up. If children normally break things rather than consider that they should put them back together, it is simply because the integrative schema of these things is inaccessible to them. On the other hand, in all households (as well as in *Headstart* or *Child Care Centers*) observers can notice how quickly most children master commercial jigsaw puzzles and can even put them together while conversing with each other, as if the puzzles were no longer a challenge. Perhaps they never were, for an organizing clue is present and can easily be picked up.

For children of that age the boundary separating the natural and social environments is blurred. A loud shout from an angry mother, or a threat from a teased sibling, or a police car siren, are both part of the natural and the human environment. A kick is as real as a table, and some words more hurtful than objects.

Hence we can expect children to enter very early on into dialogues with all sorts of people in all sorts of ways, just because they want to know, and need to know in order to direct their lives in the world and meet the unpredictable and the unknown.

Teasing is used universally as a tool to estimate the boundaries of other people's love for a child's freedom to function; it tests what the children themselves are prepared to yield to others to obtain peace and what they are prepared to fight for. Even in the last category, there are distinctions to discover; *how hard am I prepared to fight for this or that?*

How to use crying as a deliberate weapon to enlist support from parents against someone else is another dialogue, and from this a child explores justice, fairness, bias, favoritism, and so on.

Of particular interest in the area of child-adult relations is the readiness of young people to accept that adults should dictate what they, the children, do, that is, as a basis of authority. In homes where no spanking exists, or any other abuse by parents of their physical power or their economic and social know-hows, it is clear to children that some things must be done, and they obey as easily as those who are threatened. This perception of

7 Learning Other Things

one's interest as a member of a group, and the acceptance of the fact that to stop a game to eat or go out is part of the order of things, is a gift children make in the cause of family peace. To understand it as the outcome of the working of fear and a sense within the child of his own inferiority, is not to do justice to facts. Since children learn to say *no* so early, to protect themselves from pressure and to warn adults that they can create trouble, the basis of this spontaneous obedience can only be the perception of some attributes compatible with their freedom of learning which the environment has granted to them in so many areas. Children know that they are left alone to do lots of things and to grow in awareness. They know they are able to do today what they were unable to do not so long ago, and they comment on it, verbally or otherwise, very early. Their vision of the environment is balanced, one of give and take, and they know they receive a lot. They see people stop what they are doing to attend to their needs; they can be clumsy and make messes and are not necessarily scolded. Such responsiveness is part of their living and has features they can note; the recognition does not require being schooled, only awareness.

Hence, as children develop a *natural* place for themselves, reconciling balance, gravitational pulls, chains of movements, taking account of who is to occupy what portion of space, etc., they also develop a *social* place, unless distortions crop up and generate problems that could otherwise have been avoided by common sense.

Children take an astonishingly long time to learn to control their sphincters; some need years—up to 14 in some cases (this is with non-handicapped children)—even though the task seems so easy compared with the problem of learning to speak, which is normally done so rapidly. Learning sphincter control is a mixture of biological and social components, and there lies the confusion, for children and observers alike. The biological part requires only awareness. Sphincters are voluntary muscles and they are kept closed while the bladder and the rectum fill up. The additional, social part, is, when evacuation solicits the awareness, to hold them closed when otherwise they would automatically open. For months no one asked the baby to restrain himself. He was either free, like animals on a farm, to relieve himself at any moment or was given diapers to make the cleaning of the mess easier for adults. He was not required—the social demand—to learn to interfere with the release at the moment of evacuation through the accessible muscle tone of his sphincters.

It is possible that a child, because of his awareness of himself, may arrive on his own at the conclusion that such interference here and now, and only for a few moments, may save him inconveniences he himself notices—for example, that diapers are a nuisance, or that the smell of a mess or the wetness of a surface on which he wants to go on playing are unpleasant—and so enter into a dialogue through his will with these sphincters and place them under control in these circumstances. But usually the decision to do so is generated by outside sources and what a few do on their own, bed wetters do much later when sensitive to social shame (or, it could be, when capable of understanding the working of their will, which at last provides the motivation). Much later does not mean differently! The job is the same: in order to extend the duration, a certain muscle tone must be maintained at a level required by the function.

7 Learning Other Things

When small children learn to climb chairs, sofas and beds, they concentrate fully on mobilizing all they have to meet the new challenge. Intelligence as well as perception is required to find the places to hold on to, the arrangement of limbs, the muscles to affect and in what way. Children who manage to find themselves on a chair or a bed do not quite believe it (their smile of triumph is not one of complacency) and they climb down at once using gravity, therefore knowing it is an entirely different exercise than the one they are studying—and try again to climb up. Once, twice, or a few times more, and they are *certain* they have mastered this challenge. They turn to another one, which may require the new integrated skill.

What a subtle and in-depth acquaintance with one's soma is implied by the act of lifting oneself from the ground—by the act that is lumped together with other acts under the name of jumping! The first time a child feels confident that he can enter the field of jumping must be when he has deliberately synthesized the awarenesses that result from standing and walking with those that result from being lifted, from flexing muscles, etc. Intimate knowledge of his weight, and of how to increase the energy of the appropriate muscles *in toto* so as to overcome his weight, give the signal to start attempting the synthesis, virtually (that is, at the level of awareness of energy) and actually.

The virtual action of necessity precedes the actual action for there is no trial-and-error period, and none is needed. Awarenesses are available and are reachable in any detail, and a child can say to himself "I can jump" even before he has lifted himself from the floor. He has solved the problem with his somatic intelligence, that is, through the knowledge and understanding of what is involved. This work makes certain that the displacement of the right amount of energy to the proper muscles will result, in conjunction with the potential energy available in the solid floor or ground compensating his weight, in the soaring of one's body from the launching pad. Because the energy for jumping is limited, this lifting is followed by a drop to the ground, using only gravitational energy.

Each child can try again and again, as many times as the energy available in the soma permits. Some children will acknowledge that they have mastered the new skill at once; others may not believe themselves, so marvelous is the feeling of jumping, and they give themselves further chances to make sure of its presence in their battery of skills.

There is a temporal hierarchy in any act involving the soma, and learning something new never repeats what was previously learned simply because the self who engages in the next exercise has a different awareness of himself than he did before he acquired the preceding skill. It is always a different, more experienced child who attempts the next exercise; hence he makes the new challenge he gives himself into a new problem. He is bolder and he cannot be content with the same pace of progress. He does not accept a lesser task than the one he already has solved.

If he can walk forward, he wants to walk backwards. If he can walk, why not place his feet on certain marks?—and the sidewalks suddenly become inspiring because of all the lines on them. If he can jump with two feet, can he hop on one, can he hold his free leg stretched out behind him or let it hang down? Can he hop backwards or is it too hazardous? Can he take more than one step at a time climbing stairs? Or go down backwards? When will the banister become a means of going downstairs?

All these adventures, and many more, strike his imagination and solicit him to enter them.

A tacit pattern of learning emerges for each of them: cautious, marginal entry so as to explore where the stepping-stones for the activity can be found; then wholehearted investigation of the field, accepting errors as guides and putting things right immediately because the proper feedback mechanisms have been deliberately placed to monitor each activity; then further testing of the mastery of all parts of the activity before one declares oneself satisfied with what one has done. Mastery is always the aim, and this is required before the special way it is acknowledged can function—when the skill is integrated with all that was there before and the new person enters a wider challenge to test himself.

This four-part sequence of learning—*contact, analysis, mastery, application*—which ends up with an awareness of oneself owning a new power, is manifested by everybody as they acquire any skill which will become automatic after the mastery of it is acquired. (Automatic, as we know, means: that the brain has been educated to respond as needed to the special apprehension of the stimuli, and that the minimum of awareness needed to monitor the new functioning for the self is left in the psychosomatic system just constructed.)

Every child is so well acquainted with this sequence that he uses it as if it were "instinctual". But a closer look reveals the different involvements of consciousness in each of the four phases of learning. At first the self is mobilized in readiness to use everything one has and is, so that surprises from the unknown will not knock one off balance—hence the cautious, hesitant grasp of every sign so as to give oneself time for instant analysis, allowing the integration of what is safe and relevant and the filtering out of what is misleading and dangerous. As soon as one knows that the unknown has provided points of entry and one is capable of falling back on them to start again in case of a mis-step, deliberate excursions are undertaken: one goes out of one's way to find out, attempts one new thing after another in order to know whether one is in the spirit of the activity, has correct intuitions and insights into it, and can transform one's past to accommodate the new. In the transformed self is the feeling of awareness that one is more capable than before because of the new skill, and the feeling of awareness that the time given to the activity has left one owning the new skill. This feeling of harmony is the testimony to what the self calls mastery, but testing oneself as the owner of the new skill is both more precise and more acceptable to the self. So one finds the particular field that tests the possession of the skill and at once is launched on a new cycle of learning that mobilizes the whole self. And so on.

Contact with life is the generator of learning, which in turn generates more conscious life and more conscious living. Any child alive never stops being challenged by some aspect of life and displays *curiosity*—synonymous with readiness to enter a new field; *interest*—synonymous with being engaged in the activity; *enthusiasm*—synonymous with the mobilization of energy for the job on hand.

Through learning, a child becomes *more himself* (although he has used up energy in the process). He knows this himself and he gladly entertains the possibility of learning by involving himself in scores of games that seem to be ends in themselves but are in actuality the expression of the stage of the child with respect to the new activity. Games are the creation of the players, and in early childhood they are concerned with what children end up owning in the various fields of the self's expression. The motivation is clear to the player and he is attracted as long as the challenge asks him to extend himself. As soon as the challenge is seen as too easy, the game is dropped.

It is possible that one and the same game can follow the evolution of the child's successive masteries. For instance, if he has a ball and throws it, and notices that the direction in which it goes and the distance at which it falls depend on what he does, then games of throwing become of interest to him, and he happily engages in them; at first simply to give him practice with holding the ball, then in finding how the actions of his thumb, his wrist and his forearm muscles affect its direction, and later how his arm provides the energy to cover the distance.

Other games with a ball will coordinate his arms and hands so that he can catch a ball thrown at him, and for years he will practice to improve himself as a catcher.

When babies who have learned to walk want pretexts for running, they throw a ball ahead or kick it, and then run after it. Not a very amusing game indeed; it seems it cannot be fun at all. But it is greatly enjoyed by the solitary player: to give himself a reason for running he pursues a ball he has kicked!

These games that emerge spontaneously are soon added to by those which involve more than one person. Observation of young children's games will show that each partner plays his game not as a part in a collective endeavor but as if it were created and played for him alone; the others are instruments for his end. Since each is happy exploiting the others, the game can go on. But beware! If anyone does not conform to the expected pattern, he is ousted without hesitation. Game partnerships can end as abruptly as they started. Children at play are not friends, only pawns to serve the cause of each other. Shared group interest is only the appearance, not the reality. The anger of small children playing a family game when their luck is not favorable will prove this to anyone. Small children play only on their terms, mainly because their interest is neither social nor economic but concerns only what they can learn (which may be hidden from their older partners).

Brothers and sisters whose ages differ by more than about three years rarely have common interests. They play "together" only on the older's terms, and the benefit for the younger is mainly in the inspiration he obtains from his admiration of the elder's skill. As no enjoyment is possible from a game with another who is much more skilled than oneself—and children certainly attempt to be involved in their elders' games—we must accept that the pattern of the future descending into the present is clearly making its demands on such young people. What they are unable to do now, but that is nevertheless not too alien, can find its roots in a part of their functionings and provide an opening for the descent of that which needs to be realized.

It is in this sense that we hold that, through learning, one becomes *more oneself*. The potential is actualized.

But not *any* potential, only that which is ripe for realization.

This perspective brings together the facts of life, an understanding of growth in the world, a place for the co-existing generations, the shifts of consciousness from one occupation to another, the variety and the sameness of human experience on Earth.

That these diverse elements can be synthesized tells something about the truth of the vision and the validity of the instruments used in reaching it.

Seeing children as awarenesses at work, as deliberate movers in the complex inner-outer spread of the universe, seeking to grind all the forms known to other human beings into forms that the objectified self can integrate, gives us any number of entries into what we otherwise reach only as appearances.

Now, many, many details of what children have to do in order to take the place in the world that is uniquely theirs have been left out. A number of the details are already part of the arsenal of observers who have looked into this vast continent, still little chartered. Here and there some keen lover of the features of childhood has made a landing and harvested an astonishing crop. Maria Montessori and Jean Emile Marcault are among them. The first is well known as a name, but not read; the second, although one of the most profound thinkers of this century, is known to very few. They, and perhaps a few other observers, have told us that the world of childhood has to be entered on tiptoe and not with the heavy tread of laboratory technicians seeking only the confirmation of their visions; has to be entered with every tentacle and sensor alerted and not with a ready-made theory that filters out what cannot be reconciled to it: with love and respect for the person, who is as complete at every age and stage of childhood as he will be at any adult age and stage.

Indeed, love has not been looked at as a way of knowing, although all of us use it to know those we fall in love with or to know those we cannot know without it. The next chapter is devoted to this matter.

In the light of all that has been left out, readers will perhaps concede that it may have been more in their interest to have looked at some questions of childhood activity as deeply as possible than to have rushed through everything that actually happens in a child's life. As a writer, not only am I aware that I could not do justice to a field I have studied all my life, but that to try to cover it all would not serve my readers.

7 Learning Other Things

The fields of children's play and children's seeing, on which I started work in 1940, have barely been touched in this book. Likewise, I have left out singing, dancing, music making and learning to distinguish the many components of harmony, listening to stories, and the important world of symbols that mythology brings to our lives and which we need to nourish our imagination and wisdom. Each of these worthy fields calls for investigators who will genuinely attempt to understand them as they are lived by children, rather than as they should be lived according to the norms of an (improverished) adult.

In the last chapter an attempt will be made to offer readers some suggestions on how to generate an environment for children that respects their reality and provides true wealth. When we know how to serve by stepping out of the way, the incredibly efficient learning of early childhood can teach us how to help children reach further learning, just as incredibly efficient, but this time through our true care and love.

8 The Love that Babies and Young Children Need

If parents love babies without being asked, where are the signs of the feedback that informs the parents that their love is what children need?

There are two terms in the relationship. Parents do what they want, and this is said to be what their children need. But in fact babies do not know what their parents think, what to expect, and what there is to expect. Hence they do not indulge in any expectation and they act in relation to parents as they do in relation to all their other involvements.

Not being equipped to procure food for themselves, their survival depends on their being fed. They accept food and do not have to be grateful for it; so long as it is given to them, why should they think that the gift is conditional upon any form of return? Indeed, there is no such awareness in them, and men invented the notion of "maternal instinct" to place squarely on mothers the totality of the responsibility for keeping babies alive. (Cuckoos are frowned upon because they leave their eggs in the nests of other birds to avoid having to look after their offspring. Similarly, everybody considers mothers who abandon their children to be acting unnaturally.)

To find out what babies actually need in terms of love we must look beyond their survival needs. These needs include feeding, cleaning and protection against the elements (cold, excessive heat, predators, insects and pests known to be harmful, falling objects, etc.). They are clearly not the children's responsibility and can be dealt with by people who already know how to satisfy them.

The dangers associated with these needs are known by everybody except the very young, who are fearless in their innocence and, because they want to know something, can put a cockroach in their mouth or be fascinated by an avalanche coming their way. Since consciousness is engaged so thoroughly in what one needs to know, it is easy to put oneself in a situation of vulnerability to anything which is not directly apprehended. One can obviously be surprised more easily by what is not apprehended than by what one is watching.

The examination of what children need is delicate because we are engaged in looking at what is not visible. If it can be carried out, readers will see two things at once: one, why children face dangers that no one appreciates; two, why this has remained unknown for so long. Indeed, the challenge of life we are concerned with here comes because we use consciousness as an instrument for our studies and because on Earth people of all ages and levels of experience live "together."

What are the facts with which we must deal?

Each of us is engaged in his own life and knows his own concerns much more directly than he knows what others are engaged in. The superimposition of all these individual frames of references, each of which carries instruments adequate for some particular investigations but perhaps utterly useless for others, create the state of affairs we are in. Most of us, including babies, mainly comprehend what we have equipped ourselves for and what we connect with. In these areas we are more able to be alert and to respond to the impacts that reach us than in the areas for which we have little or very often no preparation.

Time structures the universe into three layers for each of us; we can cope with what involves our past, and perhaps also with our present, but we can cope with what is connected to our future only by good luck. (Here future means what *we* are not yet living even though it may be being lived by others; for example, motherhood is a possible future for baby girls.)

This state of affairs directs our examination of the love needed by babies—or, for that matter, anyone.

Adults express their love for their children by letting them judge for themselves what they need to be engaged in, according to the way the challenge strikes them, at the pace that is theirs, and until they are satisfied that they have done the job to the best of their ability, insight, and opportunities. *This is love in relation to their past and present.*

To say that, for this stage, "children know best," is no indulgence. It is simply a statement of recognition that only the child's own self is in his bag and that the outsider can only surmise the particular connection that exists between the self and its manifestations.

We already leave children alone, as a matter of course, in all areas where we have absolutely no idea what goes on—for example, during the first weeks after birth (unless we notice a disease and then attempt a remedy in our terms)—and on the whole each of us (as a child) manages quite well.

Can we do the same in areas where we have partial access? For example, when babies start to walk or run, can we love them enough to trust them rather than be anxious that they may fall and hurt themselves? Anxious love is one form of love babies do not need. A vigilant parent can be ready to assist in case of any unforeseen trouble, but keep from interfering otherwise. *Love then expresses itself in the restraint exercised by the parent upon himself.*

Children, like adults, cannot verbalize all that goes on in them all day long. Hence the environment can be informed of what goes on in a baby only if it watches, attempts to get correct insights into what children do with themselves, and then tests any hypothesis in order to be true to the requirements of the moment. *Love is expressed in these cases as respect for the child's activity.*

If it is true that adults know better in certain cases, it is still respect for truth that makes one's love intervene so as to avoid a particular danger, and intervention of this kind leaves no trauma.

Trauma is caused by the conflict of wills: parents and children wanting to assert themselves rather than, for the parent, serving the cause of growth of the child and, for the child, seeking true knowledge of his parent. Trauma is avoided by love, but love needs to be enlightened by truth. Hence parents have a criterion to help them know whether an act of their intervention is an act of love or the result of some other movement of the self.

It is true that children, for years, are smaller than their parents and that parents have powers children do not as yet have and cannot, for some time, even conceive they some day might have. This single discrepancy generates in children an inner climate of admiration that can serve their growth if adults manage to learn how to enter it and let it guide them in the parent-child relationship. The admiration is not contrived; its genuineness generates inspiration and the belief that grown-ups can do what only super-beings can do. Children naturally make their parents into heroes and omnipotent beings. This gift will last as long as the distance in power between them is a fact that is verifiable every day. The attitude rarely survives in teenagers and head-on fights between the generations may result. But even very young children can discover the lack of truth, the pretense of morally weak parents, and can suffer the shock of disillusionment, often leading to mental uncertainty and confusion.

Children do not need to concentrate on family problems; they have something else to do, more important for their true preparation for living in the complex and demanding world they were born into. But if they cannot escape being present and witnessing what is utterly incomprehensible to them, their perception and their consciousness are struck differently, and they respond in ways that may be unpredictable but fall within understandable forms. Their need for peace, so as to be able to go on with what matters to them, and their wish that the disturbing elements would vanish join to distort the functioning of their sense of truth and make them accept what they are not equipped to reject: that the world is bad, or grown-ups irrational, or God unreliable, or reality a dream, and so on.

To give up reliance on one's sense of truth is the greatest traumatism for anyone; for its guidance is needed at every moment and at all ages. The parent who knows how to respect truth and how to respect the functioning of the sense of truth in his children is giving them the love they need most, the only form that cannot be replaced by anything else. Sentimentality is, in a way, the opposite of this kind of respect. Wavering for one's own convenience also denies the consideration of truth. Truth can be taken into account rightly and more easily than any other demand in one's life. This is because we all have a sense of truth and use it from the beginning of life, knowing its functioning intimately.

8 *The Love that Babies and Young Children Need*

Parents easily mistake a thorough involvement of their children's self in the activities that are cogent to their own level of consciousness with a lack of their perception of the rest of the universe. Hence they do not take the necessary precautions to avoid situations in which their children may have to perceive what they may not comprehend, and they use the excuse of their lacking awareness when the children do not behave conveniently, irrespective of what the children are entitled to expect in accordance with their view of the harmony of their world.

The love children need most is connected with knowing the dynamics of what is immanent yet transcendental to them. To grow up normally is to bring part of the immanently transcendental to the level of the consciously mastered.

This does not mean that children do not also need the love that corresponds to the truth of feelings, but the absence of this love is less damaging to them precisely because the sturdy self of a functioning baby in contact with his sense of truth can cope with realities at his level. A loved baby will not miss a dead or absent father; he will not suffer much if he is fed the way his community feeds even if some vitamins or calories are missing; he will not mind social conditions that may later appear appalling to him: in short, he will find the environment acceptable, whatever it is. But he cannot make sense of the sometimes gentle father who becomes unpredictably violent for reasons beyond him; or of the sometimes smiling, sometimes screaming mother whose mood is governed by causes invisible to him; and so on. The universe is indeed sliced "horizontally" for him into two levels, and he is at peace in one, whatever happens, because he lives in it—it is his world; but he is totally vulnerable in the other because he does not dwell in it although he is capable of perceiving appearances in it.

For the first level, love is best expressed by considering a child as a complete person, having as much access to criteria as any other person, however old. For the second, love requires forms that distinguish adults from children and places different responsibilities on them.

Rather than ask children to obey them blindly or, at the other extreme, exercise no authority at all, parents who know that children have important jobs to do and that they cannot do them all at once will structure their relationship to their children, adopting a hands-off attitude in some sectors and a very careful and subtle involvement in others.

Humanity as a whole has lived in a way that resembles childhood life. At peace with what it knows, it fills the complement of the known universe with mystery; it experiences differently that which is transcended and that which is still transcendental. Hence the important role of religion, rituals, rites, legends and mythologies for men and women of all ages and characters.

In the case of children, in addition to all these transcendental elements there are many that belong to the realms of biology sociology, ethics, etc. It is particularly in these areas that children (but not adults) are vulnerable. In the other areas, where religion, ritual, etc., are important, children and adults are equally easily upset and love cannot do much, unless it is the love that God bestows upon humanity through all religions.

For conscious love to be effective as a vehicle carrying children into the layers of the future, each parent must develop insights of what the future contains for their children and act accordingly.

It is easy to see, for instance, that sex is transcendental for children, although perception provides entry into its appearances. Sex obviously means different things at different stages in the life of each of us and we would make a mistake in assuming that the words we use when talking of the phenomena in that field convey our meanings to young listeners. Parents who "tell everything" to their children at a certain age are amazed to find that what is retained by them in later years often either contradicts their instruction or else amounts to almost nothing.

Politicians, business people, scientists and philosophers, who open their salons to their children when their own colleagues or friends are visiting, are often baffled by the insignificance of what children glean from such sessions. Politics, economics, science and philosophy in their organized forms are transcendental to the young, who can have no access to them until a later age.

Forms that are accessible slowly gain meaning and are integrated in the self. These forms are not necessarily valid. A child and his friend can play games which are meaningful for both, but he may be misled and made into a bigot if he is given values that have no basis in truth—and made into a bigot precisely because of that. In such cases the false criteria are not seen to be false by children because the sense of truth cannot check on the validity of any criteria that are drawn from layers of experience not yet open to the functionings of the self. Without a checkable content, statements—which are only strings of words having no meaning on their own—do not gain any meaning other than as a sequence of sounds that can be repeated.

Children's sense of truth lets them know that the sounds they utter are uttered in their environment and are repeated in certain circumstances. They cannot know their meaning if it is inaccessible to them. For years they may repeat words or acts and fill them out with what meanings they choose and be totally unaware of some aspects of the meanings attached to them by the environment that the environment considers indispensable. It is for this reason that some people can become what their parents are not: what parents believe in does not strike their offspring as true.

Rebels of all kinds exist because man can hold beliefs; that is, he can accept as true what does not meet the criteria that accompany the functionings of the self. These positions can be rejected without violating one's sense of truth precisely because it was not involved in the first place; and so because of belief, there are rebels. To believe is to give reality to that which does not generate in the self the awareness that is akin to the awarenesses that the self produces when concerned only with itself, and for which it can say, "I know."

While knowing produces freedom, belief generates dependence. Hence love connected with knowing maintains autonomy and independence while attachment-love is grounded in belief.

Children need at all stages a love that leads to responsibility coupled with autonomy and independence, love that frees and is therefore joyful. To provide this love, parents need to be genuinely themselves and sensitively avoid generating experiences that throw children into the layers of consciousness where they have had no practice. Parents who are not genuinely themselves are actors all the time, and such a sustained artificiality cannot but translate itself in a hollowness that frightens the innocent child engaged in seriously living his life. If parents are not sensitive to what they generate, how can they avoid offering their offspring situations where appearances replace truth?

There are many dangers in this last situation:

1 Appearances are sometimes the truth, sometimes not, and no one can trust appearances fully, particularly when there is no access to the criteria of truth in that field.

2 Without a basis for judgment, what is one to do? Accept randomness? Guess and count on luck to be right? Lose all foundation for one's confidence in operating correctly in that field?

3 To have to continually refer to others for acceptance of one's conclusions eliminates the possibility of maintaining an integrated self.

4   In a universe in flux, where appearances cannot be trusted and the only basis for mental—and hence total—health is to be an integrated self, it is imperative to maintain the functioning of one's sense of truth all through life.

It is the role of love that moves parents to throw bridges of truth between the future and the present in their children's lives and to acknowledge that until around adolescence, they, the parents, must protect their children from being pressed by the immanent that is not yet within their children's reach. This love permits the smooth descent of the future into the present and permits meeting the unknown to be a gradual integration of what one is with what one will be. This is the correct description of the growth that has taken place since the egg was formed and therefore it reveals accurately what children are expert at doing by themselves and what they do spontaneously.

Love for a child at the beginning of his life makes parents eliminate the obstacles to his survival on the somatic level; almost all parents know how to do this, even if they need a little hint here and there. Then, as sheer survival is pushed one or two stages beneath the visible surface, parents learn to relate differently to their child, who now has other needs, and they learn to provide the psychic and spiritual environment that will make him able to cope better with the world at large. Love makes adults give up using some of their time for themselves and for their own ends and give it instead to play with their children. The games may be created only to assist their children's growth and contain no challenge to the parents, but they can have some attraction for the curious parent. A shift of view towards allowing all games a chance to school *parents* in the study of their children's functioning may make all the difference to parents' lives and to the way they knowingly serve their children. Love is needed to make that shift. It can operate by reviving in the parent a childhood attitude: the need to know—but this time to know his children as they are, here and now, and to eliminate any relationship with them based on an *a priori* model.

Parents' love makes them sensitive to the interference to the vital activities of their children caused by the social elements in the family. Clearly the running of a house makes demands on parents, who in turn are entitled to their own life. Yet that the right of parents to their own life often becomes an encroachment on the life of their children can be seen in the supremacy usually granted to dinner over all the other activities of everyone at home. Love is again needed to make a mother (or whoever has toiled to prepare dinner) see that other things are going on in the household besides the cooking of the meals. Everything must stop for dinner and everyone must rush to the table. Only love can make one see that this ritual could be the source of a distortion of reality in which one thing always subordinates all others. Further, only love can make one see that a discussion of this situation leading to a rationalization justifying the imposition of a timetable is only a rationalization and may not really serve the best interest of the members of the family. Love is needed because the total picture is difficult to see.

To say that it takes love to prepare a dinner, that love is a give-and-take, and that children must learn to give not only take, is precisely the problem for which love is needed. Only love can make one see that there may be other ways of bringing give-and-take to someone's notice than the forced acceptance of a mother's timetable, and that to call children to dinner actually demands the abandonment of what they may be engrossed in and so can generate a slow relinquishment of the respect for what other people are doing. The fact is that, at the call for dinner, whatever one is engaged in suddenly becomes unimportant compared to refueling, and the shift in focus is not a decision based on true criteria but a habit that may or may not make sense to particular children.

Love is required to be more conscious when confrontations arise. In confrontations, parents and children find their school for love. Here also are the opportunities to find out how to learn to take other people into account. Preaching and talking blur the issues. To take other people into account—as, say, policemen do—is not love. The terms must be reversed. To love *makes* one take people into account and is the method mankind has developed to transcend self-interest and give reality to the interests of others. Love makes one creative in situations that conflict with the profound knowledge that all that happens to oneself, to one's bag, is noticeable and co-extensive with reality but may not be for others. Love fertilizes one's imagination and places in oneself the presence of others as autonomous beings who are endowed with much one knows to be attributes of oneself—in particular, feelings, a will and a vision of the world. Through this love, by making oneself move to accept others, others accept oneself. The respect for their reality and all that they are engaged in is a form that love can take and a channel for its expression.

But because to love truly is demanding and to have children is not, there is no relation of cause and effect between being a parent and loving one's children, except only in the sense that animals can be said to love and protect their offspring. Even there, perhaps the only true act of love is to free the cub when he can survive by himself.

For man, love is a universe to enter and dwell in, kept intact only by the acts of will that are needed to sustain it. Parents' love is no more regulated than lovers' love. It only truly exists when it is capable of continuously renewing the vigilance that makes the other's reality never quit one's consciousness. When love is in that state it does not lose contact with this reality and does not need to be argued about. It recognizes itself while it molds itself to the ever-changing awareness of the living being one is relating to.

Children need this love and can do without all the others. To produce a humanity, a society as vast as the Earth in which all beings are equal because each is consciousness at work, this love is required. The acceptance of this love by more and more people is a measure of the movement towards humanity. Since parents and children are the people who compose the population of our world, their awakening to the fact that the love they need and the love they aspire to are one and the same, may generate in them the willingness to change so as *to be* that love—in the same sense as one *is* one's soma.

A humanity cannot exist beside or outside persons. The education of love, for love, is education of an awareness with two poles: oneself the lover and the others to be loved. When everyone loves, no one has to point the way. Things take care of themselves.

9 For the Education of the Very Young

So far this has been a book of epistemology and psychology, and it may have produced some clarification of issues for the science of knowing and the science of time. But implicit in all learning is a lesson for education, understood as the action of some people upon others. So in this chapter we shall draw some educational inferences from the studies that precede. There are many more that could be or, in other contexts, have been drawn, but we shall restrict ourselves to those that may make sense at the present social juncture when so many people are turning their attention to child care centers.

The first and most important lesson we can learn from studying the development of awareness in time, is that there are *best* moments for the presentation of opportunities to children, so that the already mobilized self can extend itself beyond what it might have done without them.

For instance, if we know how to do it, the extension of learning to speak into learning to read may take only a few moments at the age, say, of four because children on the whole may have taken themselves far enough in the study of speech to be able to make sense of the few conventions attached to writing in their language. They might then be as free and fluent in both the spoken and written languages. Another example, again if we know how to do it, would be to bring young children's awareness of both transformation and the mathematics of speech to an awareness of the mathematics of number, the study of which takes several years at present, often for little competence.

These two examples concern school subjects that traditionally tax school children, and we are saying that they could be mastered to a considerable degree before children start the first grade, providing we know how to work with actual children.

On the whole, when dealt with by professional educators, young children are lumped together and labeled as being in this or that stage of conceptualization, according to Piaget or someone else, and are therefore treated as if they had no entry into universes other than those assigned to them. Presumably all efforts at education must fit the particular stage of conceptualization they occupy. But what we have found in studying speech and its demands on very young children has shown us that children need wide nets and precise procedures to cope with language, yet they manage it very well. So well, indeed, that another language can rarely be learned as well as the first one. It is therefore a matter of adults' know-how—that is, their lack of it—that stands in the way of children learning, say, to read at an early age and not something intrinsically deficient in their mind or brain.

The exceptional child who today learns to speak at one, to read at two, to compute at three, compose music at four, etc., is a witness to the possible achievements available to young people. Such a child can teach us much and should not be set aside as a genius from whom we can learn nothing because he is so exceptional.

We must have at least one example that some learning is possible before we attempt to look into it in order to understand it and then to apply it. Then we can move from this "existence theorem" to the study of what actually makes possible an extension of a particular functioning to the point that it displays evidence of a new form.

Let us look at reading in terms of the "best" moment.

Men produced different responses when they reached the awareness that sounds could be systems of expression and communication. They then provided themselves with different forms into which to transcribe their speech but required that it remain in contact with what they knew before, that is, their speech. Once an individual finds the key to the transcription, the support of speech is then available to the visible forms and they thereby gain a totally different meaning than would otherwise meet the eye.

This movement of the mind is the answer to the challenge called *reading*. It can be made available to most children who have learned enough of the speech of their neighborhood to express themselves, and it can be made available in a matter of minutes.

What needs to be found is the phase in reading that corresponds to the talking phase in the study of speech, for only when there is an entry into the code of the transcription, will the huge equipment already available in the speaker be mobilized to carry him into the degree of fluency and comprehension of reading wished for by contemporary adults. Just as there is no need to know the totality of a spoken language before using it and just as nobody waits for a vast vocabulary before he speaks, so nobody need wait for a thorough knowledge of the code of transcription to be capable of reading.

A child proves that he can read when he is aware that a set of conventional signs, say, "as it is" can trigger a set of corresponding sounds and that these sounds, when uttered in a certain way, strangely remind one of one's spoken language. Once he can associate one more system—the system of signs—to his arsenal, which already consists of the system of meanings and the system of sounds, he finds reading as natural as speech and he forges ahead in both just as the "exceptional child" did.

Reading has little to do with the alphabet—as a correspondence of certain signs with certain sounds—and it can be learned, in the way speech was learned, without having to be dependent on more than the little that is required (and for the short time that is necessary) to assimilate the five conventions on which

9 For the Education of the Very Young

alphabetic transcription is based.* There is no need at all for memorization, there is only a need to practice the stable conventions that the inventors of the script felt were needed for the transcription of their language. The burden of memorization entailed in the usual approaches is intolerable for many children who therefore cannot be induced to do what is believed to be required but which in fact is not. These children are sometimes called immature when young, or under-achievers when older. But they still managed single-handedly the much harder job of learning to speak.

When we know how to furnish the environment with the same access to the written word as is available for the spoken word, as many children as learn to speak will learn to read, provided they can see (as, in learning to speak, they needed to hear). One can even say that they will learn to read much more easily than they learned to speak and will finish the job in a very short time—precisely because they have already learned to speak and the transition to reading demands so little.

Educationally speaking, how might this be accomplished on a large scale?

Television makes it possible to gain access to every home since people have television sets and willingly give themselves to the programs that are shown. Reading programs, like the *Pop Ups* and *Leo Color*, teaching English and Spanish respectively, when

---

* I examined these conventions in a variety of publications, among them "What We Owe Children."

seen by children enable them to make sense of the written language after only a few minutes. If the films are aired more frequently, they can induce a knowledge of reading without any additional prompting, for they have in them the evocative powers found in the processes that cause talking to become speaking.

In child care centers a mixture of approaches can make children aware that the written language can be acquired through appropriate games whose rules are definite and easily grasped because they refer, at the level of perception, to a system of signs that trigger a consistent system of sounds already owned by the children.

There is not doubt that four and five year-olds in these centers can make sense of these games and will therefore manage to learn to read. But it is likely that a number of even younger children can also be reached if they let themselves be struck by the behaviors displayed by their older companions.*

---

* As we have already observed, incidental learning is valid for all of us and is probably a big part of our overall learning. It indicates that no date can be assigned to one's arrival at any particular level of proficiency, but that there is a moment when that level is available to each learner. It also indicates that there are many entries into a field and hence, to repeat an important point, that the linear sequence teachers believe in is a fiction. Many elements that are required in order to learn a new skill may be available but, so to speak, unconscious. Only by becoming part of a new integrated whole do they show that they must have been present. Each learner displays a unique response in the way he constructs his retentions and integrations, but since after a time he gives evidence only of his mastery, which nearly everybody shows in the same way, no one suspects the uniqueness of his original solution. During learning, differences are perceptible; at the mastery stage, they are far less visible, and the illusion of one-and-the-same way of learning by everyone can find some justification—and can even lead to standardized testing. It is none the less an illusion.

Because the word "reading" has many meanings, we must clarify that we are concerned here with providing a bridge between the system of sounds already in the learner (which he has associated with the system of meanings that can and does precede it) and a system of conventional signs offered by the environment. This bridge may not suffice for the totality of the systems of sounds and signs, but it takes care of the essential connection. The rest is pure expansion and, to the child, far less challenging.

When teachers think of the extension of vocabulary as a demand of reading, they confuse two issues: new awarenesses and new words for those awarenesses. The extension must take place first in the realm of the spoken language, and if it is to be done through books, the requirements of the system of meanings eliminate the possibility of the extension being done by words alone. Pictures, diagrams or drawings are a necessity. If it is *not* done through books, experiences must be offered that lead to awarenesses to which spoken words can be associated before their written equivalents are offered.

In a child care center this extension of vocabulary can be undertaken for all children. If it is well done, there is no upper boundary to the number of words that can be added. Children are retaining systems, not memorizing tapes: the difference being that a child can take in and keep as many meanings as he can be aware of and filter out the others, while a tape is non-discriminating and holds everything. Hence it is possible for the vocabulary of children to be almost indefinitely increased, and they can employ as many new words as they find a use for in their awareness of the world.

There are no difficult words. Only relevant and irrelevant words, judged according to the functioning of one's awareness. *Helicopter, telephone, hot pants* may be more relevant to a two-year-old than *opt, apt,* and *sot* and he will integrate the former, in spite of their length, rather than the latter.

Now, before they go to school, children manage to acquire around four to six thousand words of a language which may have tens and tens of thousands. They do this by using their perception of meanings for which the environment has developed labels. But their experience goes far beyond their vocabulary, as will always be the case, because so much of life is ineffable—and, indeed, so much that might require verbal expression has not even been reached. Thus, speaking one's own language includes the use of many extra-verbal components, and child care centers can freely use the awarenesses they manifest, available to everybody from the beginning of life. The non-verbal gestures, grimaces and indications by postures or pointing, can become the source of games of recognition which may lead to verbalizations that become clues for later guidance in the world—in the language of feeling, for example, which is so much poorer than intellectual language (in the West, at least).

Several comments are needed on this point. The whole spectrum of pain is served by a small vocabulary; likewise joy, love and anger, all of whose shades of meaning are lived rather than spoken about. The spoken language is an adequate tool for concepts because they refer to classes, and language is *omnibus*, that is, to be used by all. But feelings are experienced singularly and they involve much greater amounts of energy than are involved in thoughts.

Traditional schools were founded at a time when intellectual education was highly valued by the establishment, and therefore language has been given great importance in them. Modern schools, looking more at the total person and at awarenesses, can give less stress to what is translatable into words and present experiences that, beyond a certain degree, do not even require the spoken language. If children control their behavior so that, for instance, they do not litter, make unnecessary noise, or pollute by breaking glass, because they have developed certain sensitivities, who would need proof of these awarenesses in the form of an essay or even a poster? The reduction of the importance of language does not represent a loss, and it may well be that, as a result, language will develop at a faster pace and a deeper level because far less time will be wasted in drill and repetition.

If adults understand the importance of transformation in life as a primary technique of coping with a world in flux, they will provide opportunities for far more awareness of its role in the education of children both at home and at centers or schools. This stress on change rather than stasis agrees with children's functionings and the demands of life today.

How can it be realized? The fingers of one's hands offer one example since it is possible to see that one and the same set of fingers provide a vast number of awarenesses. For instance: selecting one finger to fold over yields ten different "answers" and creates both variety and a unifying schema which ties together the set of these subsets. To fold over two at the same time multiplies the possibilities. Even if no one needs to know that there are 45 different pairs of fingers that one can choose from when folding two fingers, the fact that such a simple device can produce such awarenesses is worth noticing. Hence there are 10 different ways of showing nine fingers at once, and 45 of showing eight fingers, as consequences of what we have found out about one and two fingers. The awareness is at hand even if the language is obscure. Playing games of this sort with children of preschool age can lead them to such realizations without a word (and later to the language that will express the acquired awareness).

There is no need to study systematically all the content of such games. At one stage the children who enjoy the game of folding and unfolding fingers will meet one conclusion and some time later will meet another. After a while the results can be put together in different ways so that the children know, for example, that the numerals that are words of their language and can be used to label sets of fingers, go in pairs: that *one* and *nine, two* and *eight, three* and *seven, four* and *six, five* and *five*, all add up to each other.

Whether this conclusion is reached by children at school or at home in bed, the awareness that the same set of fingers generates the pairs (and if one knows one pair, one knows the others) links through transformation the content of the utterances, a somatic transformation resulting from one's will acting on one's muscle tone to fold over one's fingers and from an awareness of the equivalence between what is seen and what one says to describe it.

This awareness fills words with meaning and prepares for the awareness of numerical relationships, which can be developed even with some three year-olds.

Such statements, which may very likely shock both traditional and Piagetian educators, are at the basis of a renewal of education and, if given a try at child care centers or the pre-kindergarten level, will give adults a more realistic view of what can be done by young children and how to work with them to help them.

Too often the concept that children only understand manipulative materials and fail to grasp "the abstract" has been taken on faith. That they prefer to act on materials and transform what is given, rather than relate to arbitrary requests from adults who do not know how to make sense to them, is to be welcomed—but only as a second best. The inclinations and powers of children of one or two years old are shown in their spontaneous and successful attempt to crack the code of the spoken language of their environment. If anything is "abstract," is it not the set of words of any language? Is there a reality in a "train" made of rods? Is there not abstraction in looking at the length of rods while seeing their volume and their surfaces? Is there not intellectual flexibility in saying "two" for "one and one" and conversely? Educators have *not* given children a chance. Nor even themselves, really. For if they had, they would have found what is there to be found: that the intellectual powers of pre-school children are a testimony to their real powers and that to educate these powers means to take children beyond the level they are at when they come to them.

In my book *Towards a Visual Culture* I spelled out how a number of particular exercises can be made into films. They could have found a place in this chapter with the suggestion that they be performed in front of the children as if the cameras were there to record the performance for the intended films. All these exercises are about awareness and are intended for children of pre-school age. Perhaps readers of this book will refer to them to add to their arsenal of games to help children reach awarenesses that their environment may not present to them.

The visual character of all these exercises or games permits one to by-pass the difficulties that words put in the way. The games do not lead to scholastic knowledge, but they allow every child to know himself much better and, indeed, to find in his awareness criteria that serve him much better than knowledge of the kind transmitted by instruction ever can. After playing these games so many know-hows are available to a child that whenever verbalization is possible their reality will be made plain to anyone in the environment. But even when verbalization is not possible, each child will nonetheless be equipped to meet much more of the world than educators who patronize him dare present.

Instead of letting children "experience" sand and water, or this and that, as if they were poor things knowing so little, when we see their selves and their awarenesses as beacons, we find that their universe is lit from inside and made sense of in unpredictable and profound fashions. The true relationship of the self to the world takes the form that will make the world yield up some secret, which then becomes an explicit know-how known only to one's self and useable by it.

When a child is given an unknown box to open he has no memory of how to do it; he uses initiative to make the box yield its secret, and he starts a number of dialogues until he either gives up, having found his present resources wanting, or he contemplates the open box and verbally, or otherwise, concludes: "It was easy!"

This kind of experiencing is educational in that the self finds itself more competent at the end of the investigation with respect to the activities concerned, even though no word has been added to one's vocabulary, and no statement has been made to sum up the use of one's time.

In child care centers, a child's incidental learning may lead to acquaintances with himself far more important than those gained through scholastic knowledge. To refine his hearing through listening to all sorts of sounds and to learn to recognize which sound is produced by what source and be certain of the connection is equipping his self for the future and enabling his brain to provide feedback mechanisms that can inform his self about this field from now on.

Education of awareness is the only possible and the only worthwhile education. Whenever we meet an educated person, we meet someone who has done something to himself so that the world around him is full of meaning for him and whose perceptions trigger the correct response to cope with all the messages that reach the self. When we meet a child who has learned to speak, we meet such an educated person, one who has done with speech what can be done in scores of other fields. So we can say: one *knows* how to speak; speech is a power one owns from now on.

Early childhood education can provide each child with extended powers and the awareness of what can be done with these powers. The new pedagogy, which is based on awareness, can help in the designing of schools or centers, in the designing of equipment, in the designing of a schedule that provides young children with opportunities in many fields which together may permit an all-round education as thorough as that given by every child to himself in the fields we have studied in the earlier chapters.

Each of us has been by far the best teacher each of us has had.

Can we not learn from these examples how to educate mankind towards making itself a sensible user of the enormous potential in each of us, barely suspected even in the case of those among us we acknowledge as exceptional?

The overall educational conclusion from this book is that since we have barely started subordinating teaching to learning, because we only recently started to study learning in man, we can look forward to a fertile period of educational renewal that will bring to each inhabitant of the Earth the benefits of being thoroughly human.

Further Reading

Ideas and insights made explicit in this book may be seen in greater relief if the following texts by the same author are consulted:

- *What We Owe Children*
- *Towards a Visual Culture*
- *The Adolescent and His Will*
- *Un Nouveau Phénomène Psychosomatique*
- *Conscience de la Conscience*

Specific teaching materials, incorporating the results of the author's studies, are available under the following names:

- *Words in Color (for teaching reading)*
- *Mathematics with Algebricks*
- *Folklore of Mathematics (films)*
- *The Silent Way (for teaching foreign languages)*

All these materials, and others, are obtainable from Educational Solutions Inc., www.EducationalSolutions.com.

www.ingramcontent.com/pod-product-compliance
Lightning Source LLC
Chambersburg PA
CBHW080543170426
43195CB00016B/2664